WRESTLING BABYLON

Piledriving Tales of Drugs, Sex, Death, and Scandal

IRVIN MUCHNICK

ECW Press

Published by ECW PRESS
2120 Queen Street East, Suite 200, Toronto, Ontario, Canada M4E 1E2

LIBRARY AND ARCHIVES CANADA CATALOGUING IN PUBLICATION

Muchnick, Irvin
Wrestling Babylon : piledriving tales of drugs, sex,
death, and scandal / Irvin Muchnick.

ISBN-13: 978-1-55022-761-1
ISBN-10: 1-55022-761-0

1. Wrestling. 2. Wrestling—Social aspects. I. Title.

GV1195.M82 2007   796.812   C2006-906798-8

Editor: Michael Holmes
Cover and Text Design: Tania Craan
Production: Mary Bowness
Printing: Thomson-Shore

Second Printing

This book is set in Minion and Akzidenz Grotesk

DISTRIBUTION
CANADA: Jaguar Book Group, 100 Armstrong Ave., Georgetown, ON L7G 5S4
UNITED STATES: Independent Publishers Group, 814 North Franklin St.,
Chicago, IL 60610

PRINTED AND BOUND IN THE UNITED STATES

ECW PRESS
ecwpress.com

for my parents
Simon Muchnick (1918-2004)
Esther Mildred Figus Muchnick (1920-2005)

The people that once bestowed commands, consulships, legions,
and all else, now concerns itself no more, and longs eagerly
for just two things — bread and circuses!

— JUVENAL

CONTENTS

IT'S A WWE WORLD, THE REST OF US ARE JUST LIVING IN IT

FOREWORD

by Bert Randolph Sugar

I met Irvin Muchnick, the author of this book, on the 44th floor of the World Trade Center back in 1985 at a hearing conducted by a state senator named Abraham Bernstein to investigate whether professional wrestling should be banned in New York State. I was hustling a book that had just been published about the latest "wrestling renaissance" — one of dozens of books I've had the pleasure of penning on all manner of American sport and folly. Irv, for his part, was hustling a book that had yet to be published. Bill Geist (now a correspondent for *CBS Sunday Morning*) was writing a comedy column about the hearing for *The New York Times*.

Irv got to Geist first with a quote to the effect that Senator Bernstein was behaving like the Grinch Who Stole Christmas. Never known to suffer from a loss of words, I sucked my thumb and told Geist: "I know how it's going to end when I see *Hamlet*, too, but I still go to the theater to watch Olivier."

Here we are two-plus decades later, and the World Trade Center is no more, but I'm delighted to be calling attention to Irv Muchnick's powerful pieces on grossly undercovered aspects of pro wrestling behind the scenes. This is an industry with as much to say about our collective consciousness as ballet, opera, and athletics combined — and with *Wrestling Babylon* it has met its match. A few hundred years from now some archeologist is going to dig up a copy, alongside a box of men's neckties, and wonder which aspect of our culture was stranger.

Irv is a nephew of another modest person, but also a formidable figure in wrestling history: long-time St. Louis promoter and National Wrestling Alliance president Sam Muchnick. And though Irv would never put it quite this way himself, let me say that he is truly a writer ahead of his times. In 1991 he talked *Spy* magazine into letting him write a thousand words about the backstage war in bodybuilding, where wrestling honcho Vince McMahon was trying to horn in on the turf of Joe Weider. A few months later the editors wound up giving Irv an extra 3,000 words and putting the story on the cover. This was seven years before McMahon and Martha Stewart issued public stock offerings on Wall Street in the same week. That *Spy* magazine would soon go the way of Ted Turner's World Championship Wrestling — in other words, into oblivion — is beside the point.

Proving his versatility, Irv has put more than one magazine out of business. In between exposing the Von Erich wrestling family for *Penthouse* (a story selected for the book *Best Magazine Articles: 1988*) and retailing naughty outside-the-ring anecdotes for a short-lived online publication of New York's Museum of Sex, he profiled a maverick college professor for *Lingua Franca*, which at the time was the *Ring* magazine of academia. His writings reveal the tension between his impressive talent and his slumming instincts. He would be the first to tell you that he has never quite gotten a toehold in the mainstream publishing world, but maybe he likes it that way. His own writer and his own man, he sprinkles his findings at intervals, like Smokey the Bear on fire prevention. (That one is from Charles Einstein, the baseball anthologist; along with Irv and Milton Berle, I know a good line when I steal it.)

Call Muchnick vulgar if you must, but it's a hard charge to make stick because his prose is too elegant. Besides, he revels in the characterization, every bit as much as I enjoy being pegged "Runyonesque." (You could look it up in Wikipedia.) Quoting

Bill Veeck — whom he wrote about and befriended late in Veeck's life — Irv points out that the Latin root of "vulgar" is *vulgaris*, which means "of the people." In his heart of hearts Irv will always be a midwestern populist who spent his adult life exiled on two coasts. "Part of me would dearly love to return to the United States of America," he says, "but I know it will never happen."

Still, Irv is a man on a mission. For a time he served as assistant director of the National Writers Union and started a rights-clearance agency that modeled for authors in new technologies what ASCAP has done for creators in the music business. He later became a consultant, in which capacity he more or less invented class-action copyright litigation on behalf of writers. When the lawyers and plaintiffs of one of his stepchildren suits went into the tank for publishers, Irv spearheaded objections to the settlement and took the case up to appellate courts. Somehow along the way he and his long-suffering wife have found time to raise four children in the People's Republic of Berkeley, California, the Madison Square Garden of political theater. According to Irv, Yeats said we all have to choose between perfection of the art and of the life.

And now ECW PRESS has chosen the perfect vehicle — and done all of us a service — by collecting Muchnick's writings on wrestling. The result is a wacky marriage of author and subject, form and function, lowbrow and no-brow. In a world of timid, formulaic scrivenings on sports and entertainment and sports entertainment, *Wrestling Babylon* is a sock on the jaw.

Hardcore legend Mick Foley as Cactus Jack

INTRODUCTION

Readers of these lovingly assembled stories will be interested to know that they were supported by just a handful of conversations over the years with Vince McMahon himself, master of the contemporary pro wrestling universe, for whom the viewpoint herein serves as a kind of Greek chorus.

It's human nature to stoke fantasies of prowess, inside and outside the squared circle; I confess that one of mine is speculating that I might be taken seriously enough to conjure a metaphor from classical antiquity, even if it's an attenuated one, like "Greek chorus." Wasn't Jacques Barzun the windbag who wrote, "Whoever wants to know the heart and mind of America had better learn baseball"? Well, when my own sorry ass is laid to rest, I want the epitaph to read: "The unenviable calling of Irvin [not Ervin, not Irwin, not Ivan] Muchnick [not Mushnick, not Munchnick, not Muchnik] was to document the correlation between the popularity of pro wrestling and larger societal forces in the silver age of the American empire."

Or something like that. According to Archimedes, all you need is a place to stand and you can move the earth. Wrestling, for better or for worse, is where my career stands. To be precise, where it wobbles, like Cactus Jack at the top of a cage.

I'll just have to hope this indelible literary legacy isn't further complicated by the fact that only one of my few chats with "Mr." McMahon had much substance. That was my interview of him for *People* magazine in March of 1992, when a harried Vince, on a cell phone backstage in Mobile, Alabama, during the taping of the key last set of television shows prior to *WrestleMania VIII*, worked to extinguish the brushfire that had engulfed his top star, Hulk Hogan, the subject of an article headed to press.

The *People* story — based on information from, among others, some of Hogan's former wrestling running mates, including "Dr. D" David Shults, Superstar Billy Graham, Billy Jack Haynes, and Randy Culley — exposed the poorly kept secret that the Hulkster, perhaps history's highest-hairlined kiddie cartoon hero, was a longtime abuser of anabolic steroids. (The article is reprinted as Chapter 7 of this volume.) The previous year, Hogan's lawyer had succeeded in getting him out of testifying at the trial of George Zahorian, the McMahon-connected, Pennsylvania State Athletic Commission-appointed attending physician at wrestling shows staged within driving distance of Zahorian's Harrisburg medical clinic, where he was well known to procure and dispense steroids like candy. This fateful nexus of circumstances landed the good doctor in federal prison for violating a recently enacted statute that criminalized the prescription of steroids for non-therapeutic purposes.

If the scenario sounds quaint, you must remember that it would be another decade before a baseball star, Rafael Palmeiro (himself subsequently involved in a steroid scandal), appeared on TV commercials urging men to "step up to the plate" and talk frankly with their doctors about Viagra. In wartime, they like to say that partisanship ends at the water's edge, and the same is true for the relationship between libertarianism and image-making. Wrestling is all about image — war by other means.

Back in 1991, Hogan proceeded to make matters worse by going on the Arsenio Hall talk show after the Zahorian trial and lying through his teeth; Hulk maintained that his freakish physique was purely the product of his patent-pending formula of prayers and vitamins. Disgruntled ex-associates thereupon sniffed the potential profit in going on the record *au contraire*, and journalists piled on like the pack of jackals we are. A stringer for *People*'s San Francisco bureau, I'd been pitching a Hulk whistleblower for months, but I didn't get a green light until word reached the editors that the *Los Angeles Times* was readying a similar piece.

That's why McMahon, after almost a week of ignoring requests for comment, was on the phone with me on deadline. His mission: to ward off death by tabloid torture.

In those days, at least, Vince famously kept his fingerprints all over his promotion's important storylines. And no "angles" were more important than the final fine hype brushstrokes in the run-up to *WrestleMania*, that annual pay-per-view extravaganza which, echoing the Super Bowl, was sequenced with mythopoeic Roman numerals. He therefore could be forgiven for the occasional distraction or disorientation. More than once he addressed me as "Phil" — evidently confusing me with *New York Post* columnist and McMahon basher Phil Mushnick.

Dr D. David Shults

But multitasking and all, Vince remained, on the whole, lucid under stress, admirably so. His general mien was professional but he also flashed his legendary combativeness. At one point I asked how much his company, then called TitanSports, and its insurer had had to fork over in 1985 to settle a lawsuit by John Stossel (the ABC 20/20 correspondent whom David Shults slapped silly on camera when Stossel confronted him with the hoary and boring question, "Is it fake?"). McMahon said he didn't remember the amount. I said it wasn't credible for a CEO not to remember such a hefty sum, believed to be about $425,000.

"Please don't insult me," Vince replied evenly. "I said *I don't re-member.*"

I was impressed despite myself. Before ringing off, I thanked McMahon for his time and allowed that I considered him one of the most brilliant businessmen of our era. Through the static-plagued wireless connection, you could practically hear his rubbery features stretch into a beam, his barrel chest pump as though he'd just done a dozen reps of a bench press.

"I appreciate that," he said, and turned reflective. "Nothing gives me more pleasure than when a family writes in to say that they attended one of our shows and were entertained by it. That's what we do. It's our passion."

There are two known kinds of wrestling writers and several sub-species. You can decide for yourself whether I belong to any of them.

First, there are people suffering from enlarged earnest nodes. Now, I'm a soft-core fan myself, but let's face it, some of these folks are stone-cold stupid. On my personal spectrum, however, they are not as obnoxious as those who pander to their stupidity, such as 20/20's Stossel. The symptoms of journalists diagnosed with advanced-stage Stosselism don't stop at garden-variety ig-norance or faux naiveté; they run the gamut all the way to stunning, full-blown, preternatural witlessness. Had Dr. Zahorian examined them prior to a World Wrestling Federation

TV shoot in Allentown circa 1983, they surely would have been told to take two irony pills and call back in the morning.

In another major camp reside the Deconstructionists. For them, every sneer of Hunter Hearst Helmsley (not to mention whether Triple H kisses Stephanie McMahon chastely or with deep-tonguing) contains elusive code. The task of cracking this code falls alternately to Johnny-come-lately sociologists and to obsessed chroniclers who serve the same role for the "serious and thoughtful" fan community that Kremlinologists do for the Council on Foreign Relations crowd.

Once more unto this breach steps the humble wordsmith of the present collection. I've always had a limit for how long I can sit around like a character in *This Is Spinal Tap*, a parody of a parody, pondering the nuances in the oeuvres of Moby Grape and T. Rex. And so I submit for your approval a revolutionary concept: reportage and analysis on wrestling with Zen balance.

Note that the definitions of these categories nowhere account for specific knowledge of the subject per se. If I were paid royalties for every time I conceded that Dave Meltzer, publisher of the *Wrestling Observer Newsletter*, had forgotten more about wrestling than I'll ever know, then I could retire to the beach at Nice, home of Rene Goulet (or was that Sergeant Jacques Goulet of the French Foreign Legion?). You see, wrestling is the ultimate egalitarian pastime. In contrast even with boxing — the "sweet science," whose industrial essence is uncomfortably contiguous to wrestling's but that's a subject for another day — highbrows need not apply. One's critique of wrestling is little more than how one responds viscerally to what the eggheads atomize into its "performance art elements."

What's more, wrestling gimmickry evolves. Once upon a time they had a thing called a "fence match" to blow off feuds — the ring would be surrounded by the sort of barrier commonly found between sleepy suburban tracts, and ultimately the paraphernalia had almost no impact on the staging of the match. (This stipulation was supposedly meant to handicap antagonists who did their most effective work outside the ropes.) Today there are barbed-wire-steel-cage-I-quit-coal-miner's-glove-pole-ladder matches, with the props in the foreground, characters in their own right, drawn to the destiny of the outcome.

Sure, if you're going to comment on wrestling while pretending to be super-hip, then tone-deafness with respect to tradition and background and context will come back to bite you. But the point is that it's not a matter of credentials, or mastery of data at the box-score level. My own house is a cable-free zone; the programming in that medium is deemed . . . inconsistent with our family's child-rearing philosophy. But does that disqualify me from writing about wrestling? Hardly. Plot progression in wrestling is a lot like that in Russian literature, which is to say not very important at all. Scratch a Dostoevsky or Gogol short story at almost any point on its surface and you will get a quick grasp of its fundamentals. Similarly, when we're at a hotel on vacation, a flick of the wrist on the remote control activates the "refresh" button on the season's wrestling angles as effortlessly as my wife (who works full-time) can catch up with daytime soap operas. For research purposes, this method generates efficiency. And it has the bonus of disarming my dear wife, whose tendency to go into high moral dudgeon is mitigated by the indulgence of her own pleasures, innocent and otherwise.

Turning to the content of the genre itself, I suspect my tastes are atypical. Again, I don't hold this up as a social virtue, I simply report it. Maybe that's how we all feel about our specific likes and dislikes. Anyway, there's consensus that blood fascinates, or downright excites. Bruiser Brody and Mick Foley were two of the more interesting wrestling minds of the last generation. Neither could be accused of being a non-intellectual, yet both nursed out-and-out "juice" fetishes. But that stuff still grosses me out.

I'll go even further. Across all these decades, what is often presented as wrestling's basic paradigm — catharsis, adrenaline rush — is not its main attraction for me, at least so far as I'm conscious of it. Controlled violence, not can-you-top-this brutality,

The original ECW of the 1990s was a promotion that maxed out on bloodlust

is what triggers something deep. (Deep as in "extending far inward," not deep as in "profound.") It's the difference between Batman and Superman. At its core is something dreamlike, something faintly — hell, *explicitly* — erotic.

Pornography, in other words. But only of the spirit. Paging Dr. Freud . . .

The articles that comprise *Wrestling Babylon* are not presented in chronological order. If they were, they would have a different anthropological value. When I first started doing this, whatever "this" is, there was literally zero market for non-cartoonish writing about any aspect of pro wrestling in a semi-serious magazine. Once such a market was isolated, assumptions were still taboo. Even an article on regulation by state agencies — a topic with a built-in laugh track — required straight-faced explanations of wrestling's most ludicrous elements, according to my editor at *The Washington Monthly*, a young Matthew Cooper (now White House correspondent at *Time*, and one of the journalists who was leaked the name of CIA agent Valery Plame, the wife of Bush administration critic Joseph Wilson).

Promoting this piece on National Public Radio's *Fresh Air*, I was asked by interviewer par excellence Terry Gross whether the stuff was real. "No, Virginia, pro wrestling is not the epitome of the Greco-Roman tradition," I said, and elaborated. I chose to start off elliptically, not because I worried about exposing the business, or as insiders call it, "breaking kayfabe," but because coy answers to obvious questions exercise mental muscles. This in turn prevents early-onset Stosselism.

Then there's the issue of the overthrow of the old order, of which I was a presumed defender by bloodline. (See Chapter 1, "Sam Muchnick to Vince McMahon.") Did I oppose the WWFization of wrestling? You bet I did. Why? Beats the hell out of me. It seemed important at the time, though I can't really identify what discrete principle was at stake.

As the marketing war in wrestling wore on, and as Vince McMahon tossed one adversary after another over the top rope like so many jabroneys, each more formidable than the last — not just old-school buffoons like Verne Gagne and Jim Crockett, but also TV titans like Eddie Einhorn and Ted Turner — a larger narrative took shape. The story wasn't one of heroes and villains. The story, rather, was that wrestling obviously *did* have the same DNA structure as other American sports. And this became apparent not because wrestling started to look more legit (unless you counted the revenue). It became apparent because *legit sports started to look more and more like wrestling*. With each passing year the former's vehicles of hype, which used to be on the extracurricular extremes, are more and more central to the latter, as well. Tasteless non sequitur promos, performance- and physique-enhancing drugs, the triumph of "attitude" over substance — you name it, you want it, you got it.

Eighteenth century historian Edward Gibbon had a field day showing how the same phenomenon of decadence-by-osmosis afflicted the Romans. Today, trendy commentators are quick to seize the pertinent analogies — the lions and the Christians yadda yadda yadda — whenever the "wrestling renaissance" drops, ever so briefly, onto their radar screens. But these pillars of the community are too establishment, too domestic, too beholden to mainstream sports and media, to pick up on the delicious moral and ethical and behavioral curlicues and switchbacks along the mountain road. With prodding, they do grasp the idea that a demimonde morphed into a juggernaut. What they miss is that their own secure, respectable forms of "sports entertainment" are converging upon wrestling, like the pigs and the men at the end of *Animal Farm*.

Above all, I believe, these bloviators lack the requisite solid information to inject their pontifications with credibility. To put it bluntly, they fake it. There I go again, contradicting myself: specific knowledge *does* count for something. Specific knowledge combined with a non-dumbed-down P.O.V.

Thus was born a niche. Consumers unfamiliar with the process think writers choose their subjects. Bull — it's the other way around. Do you honestly believe that I wouldn't, in a heartbeat, be cranking out high-toned novels about the interior lives of horny professors if such fodder was, in any way, shape, or form, anywhere in my genetic makeup?

I give you the only alternative my meager powers can summon. Read and enjoy. To quote the maverick baseball owner Bill Veeck: "Look for me under the arc lights, boys, I'll be back. . . ."

Hogan: before Hulkamania ran wild

THE WAY IT WAS

Sam Muchnick

CHAPTER 1

SAM MUCHNICK TO VINCE McMAHON

How Wrestling Got a Hold on My Uncle and the Nation

On the evening of Friday, November 22, 1963, Monsignor Louis Meyer of Epiphany of Our Lord Parish, director of the youth department for the Archdiocese of St. Louis, read a prayer in memory of President John F. Kennedy, who had died less than eight hours earlier in Dallas from an assassin's bullets.

The 7,200 people filling two-thirds of the seats at Kiel Auditorium stood in respectful silence as the priest eulogized their martyred leader. When Monsignor Meyer was finished, everyone turned toward the American flag onstage while the U.S. Army Band Chorus recording of the national anthem blared tinnily over the public-address system. Then the crowd settled in for a night of professional wrestling, climaxed by National Wrestling Alliance heavyweight champion Lou Thesz's title defense against the evil German, Fritz Von Erich.

Two days later, the commissioner of the National Football League, Pete Rozelle, would be excoriated for ordering NFL teams to play their full slate of games while the nation was still reeling from the death of the president. Yet in St. Louis there was no particular outcry when the NWA's show went forward. If anything, the promoter won sympathy for his predicament — after all, most of the wrestlers had already arrived in town before news of the assassination — and praise for his ingenuity in arranging a prayerful preamble to the ritual of mayhem performed by assorted eccentric, underdressed circus athletes.

Why?

I believe I know some of the answers to that question — in part because I myself, at age nine, was in attendance at Kiel Auditorium that night. Also because the St. Louis promoter was my late uncle, Sam Muchnick.

A jagged line running from Sam Muchnick, the principal owner of the St. Louis Wrestling Club, to Vincent Kennedy McMahon, the flamboyant chairman of World Wrestling Entertainment, tells a

LOUIS THESZ
World's Champion
Wrestler

BERT'S
K.C.

good slice of what might be called the backstory of twentieth century popular culture.

McMahon turned wrestling into more than just a compelling metaphor for the mountebank inside all of us. For better or worse, the WWE is a powerful fact on the ground of our national life — providing the theme for a Times Square entertainment complex, churning out bestselling autobiographies, underpinning a huge public stock offering, helping elect a governor and manufacture one of the movie industry's hottest action stars, and cheerfully exporting teen-male misogyny from cable fringe to network prime time.

American sports and society had an appointment with McMahon's XFL football on NBC on Saturday nights in 2001. That that experiment would go down as one of the most spectacular failures in television history shouldn't obscure the meaning of its having happened at all. The XFL was an all-too-glibly dismissed footprint of the mainstreaming of antisocial values. With or without the XFL, Vince McMahon became a showbiz baron, a *Forbes* 400 billionaire, and like his Connecticut forebear P.T. Barnum, an A-list exhibit to H.L. Mencken's contention that no one ever went broke underestimating the intelligence of the masses.

In the World According to Vince — that meta-reality with unassailable traction — the XFL story contained no moral, unless it was that his brilliance in one field didn't necessarily translate into another. In truth, this was a lesson he'd learned well before he owned wrestling — as far back as 1974, when his promotion of a continent-wide live closed-circuit telecast of an Evel Knievel stunt event flopped worse than Knievel's motorcycle sinking safely attached to a parachute down into Idaho's Snake River Canyon gorge.

And it was a lesson McMahon saw reinforced at least three other times after he had become master of the wrestling universe — when his company, feeling its oats, made failed forays into the movie business, boxing, and bodybuilding. (One area's genius, it seems, is another's "mark.") Asked by television interviewer Bob

Costas, in the midst of the XFL debacle, what he would do if his dream of a football league died hard, as it would swiftly proceed to do, McMahon replied defiantly, and with a lack of sentimentality that you had to admire at some level. "I'll get up off my kiester and try something else," he snarled.

My Uncle Sam, too, was quite successful, on his own scale and his own terms. He preferred operating in the shadows instead of in the spotlight. For him, respectability was something to be finessed and molded, rather than just turned on its head and overwhelmed by capital, so he guarded exposure as zealously as McMahon would court it.

But in the final analysis, and like it or not, the two men of two generations were bonded by the gimmickry of their product, by their slippery quest for legitimacy, and by the even more disturbing sense that their authenticity revealed our dishonesty, rather than the other way around. Verisimilitude, not truth, was the coin of their realm.

Larry Matysik interviews Bruiser Brody

Like the early moguls of Hollywood — Louis B. Mayer, Jack Warner, Samuel Goldwyn — some of the impresarios most responsible for transforming wrestling from country carnival sideshow to urban arena spectacle happened to be Jews from Eastern Europe. Sam Muchnick was born in the Ukraine in 1905. Another wrestling promoter with roots in the Pale of Settlement was Jack Pfefer, a Russian whose thick Yiddish accent and stereotypical money manipulations were the stuff of legend — reviled legend.

Sam's model was different, smoother, more assimilated. I always thought of Sammy Glick, the fast-talking deal-maker of Budd Shulberg's novel *What Makes Sammy Run?*, though the Sammy I knew exuded less hyperkinetic insecurity and more sedentary mystique. My father's father was a man of religion who had a hard time holding down a job in America because he refused to work on the Sabbath. Uncle Sam, like Sammy Glick, would have none of that, and quickly jettisoned religion, accent, and other old-world baggage.

But unlike Jack Pfefer, or for that matter, just about any wrestling promoter of any era or ethnicity, Sam was known to be scrupulously, almost fetishistically, honest in his business dealings. His last aide de camp, Larry Matysik, had a strict routine after every show, which involved breaking down 32 percent of the house gate receipts into cash envelopes, scaled from the main-eventers (who shared a full half of the 32 percent) on down to the "job boy" in the first preliminary match. Often the distribution was completed before the wrestlers had finished showering. In 1953 an electricians' union strike forced the late cancellation of a St. Louis wrestling show. Sam gathered the talent and explained what had happened before proceeding to pay each man a generous estimate of what might have been his share of the house that never was. The wrestlers, led by a guy named Hans Schmidt, caucused, and Schmidt soon returned, handing every dime back to Sam.

"We decided we don't even want trans," Schmidt said. "You've always treated us fair and square, and the electricians' strike isn't your fault." Fortunately for Hans Schmidt's reputation as a German heel, this anecdote didn't leak to the public.

Upon graduation from Central High School in St. Louis, Sam helped support his immigrant family with a job at the post office. In 1926 he got his first big break, joining the sports department of the *St. Louis Times*. Sam lacked the writing polish of his Cardinals baseball beat colleague, Notre Dame-educated Walter W. (Red) Smith of the *St. Louis Star*, later a Pulitzer Prize–winning columnist in New York. But in a time of Prohibition and of baseball idol Babe Ruth's discreetly unreported debaucheries, no journalist could schmooze better or hold secrets closer than the man known affectionately as "Thammy" (a reference to his signature lisp). Along the way, Sam befriended Jack Dempsey, Mae West, and Al Capone. Among the guys and dolls, Sam Muchnick was a guy's guy. His crowd specialized in practical jokes that in the abstract were funny, but in the retelling sound creepily sadistic — such as the time he lent his car to his best friend, wrestler Ray Steele, and then arranged to have Steele thrown in the pokey overnight for stealing it.

A facility at these kinds of head games would come in handy after the *Times* went under in 1932 and Sam landed as the publicist and right-hand man for Tom Packs, a St. Louis-based circus entrepreneur who was also one of a handful of promoters running the nascent national pro-wrestling "syndicate." Eventually the two had a falling out and Sam started his own promotion.

The golden age of wrestling, coinciding with the advent of television and the formation of a consortium of promoters called the National Wrestling Alliance, followed Sam's service during World War II in the Panama Canal Zone. An Army buddy, Mel Price, also a former sportswriter, who had been elected to Congress from the East St. Louis, Illinois, district, proved an invaluable ally when the NWA, your basic cartel, got investigated by the Justice Department.

Promoter potentates at a National Wrestling Alliance convention

Price — who would go on to become the longtime chairman of the House Armed Services Committee — helped negotiate a consent decree whereby the NWA continued to operate despite few if any changes to its anti-competitive practices.

The wrestling nation was thus safely divided into Mafia-like fiefdoms, with each promoter running things pretty much his own way. The only unifying principle was the touring NWA champion, who through much of that period was another St. Louis product, Lou Thesz, the son of a Hungarian shoemaker. (When Thesz died in 2002, his obituary made *The New York Times*.) Sam Muchnick was a founder of the NWA and, with only a couple of brief interregnums, the organization's president for a quarter of a century.

Vince McMahon's WWE sells real theater. Sam Muchnick's NWA sold fake sport. While there's no accounting for taste, aficionados swear that this is a distinction with a difference.

But let's dispense with the sentimental notion that what McMahon corrupted was anything other than a conceit, with the emphasis on the "con." Pro wrestling has been fixed since the earliest days of Strangler Lewis, Farmer Burns, and Frank Gotch, and for the simplest possible reason: While the amateur version of the sport appeals to something primal in us, it achieves critical market mass only when wed to a storyline. Wrestlers used to weave their narrative strictly between the ropes via a lowbrow performance art known as "working." The "spots," whether high-wire maneuvers like flying dropkicks, or pulled punches or more basic mat moves, were communicated by whispers and body language. If a worker got out of line and attempted a "double-cross," his opponent was expected to "shoot" or "hook" to bring about the intended result. (However, such a breach of etiquette was rare.) Up and down the "rasslers" would go, suspending the breath, emotions, and disbelief of the spectators of a slower-paced era.

McMahon merely took wrestling apocrypha to a heady new level, much the way Michael Milken shook the financial world with the invention of junk bonds. The fact that there are now re-takes of botched interviews before live audiences who are instantly let in on the joke is essentially an esthetic evolution. McMahon is a postmodernist whose historical role, more than anything else, is to put pretense in its place, for fans and non-fans alike. As he has proven, the carny code of "kayfabe" — whereby even the most sophisticated observers might not catch on to the broad outlines of the charade — was more about the psychological needs of the workers than about the business fallout of disillusioning the "marks."

Still, one conclusion is inescapable. Wrestlers from the old school, who had their hands full with their campy struggle to maintain credibility before camp was cool, took care of each other in the ring. They suffered from ordinary sports injuries and cauliflower ears, but they also by and large led long and productive, if somewhat crusty and Runyonesque, lives. A few even had crossover careers — and I'm not just talking about Gorgeous George. Check out Mike Mazurki in the 1949 Richard

New Jack: as hard-core as it gets

Widmark–Gene Tierney noir classic *Night and the City*, one of Mazurki's numerous character roles in the forties and fifties. Contemporary wrestlers might snicker at the hokum, but their ironic distance from the art of the work exacts a considerable physical and psychic cost. As the tortured comparisons to the Greco-Roman tradition have declined, so the ante for hard-core realism has been upped. Today, wrestlers bash each other over the head with chairs or ram each other into cars offstage, crash onto thumbtacks from ladders or steel cages, pump themselves with steroids and human growth hormone, snort cocaine, pop uppers and downers, and, not incidentally, drop dead before their time in alarming numbers. As my friend Phil Mushnick of the *New York Post* once wrote, you won't find a lot of Old Timers' Days in pro wrestling.

Vince McMahon's special genius as a businessman is his ability to generate multiple revenue streams; on the financial news circuit, his wife and CEO Linda McMahon assures New York Stock

Exchange investors that the company is always looking for "new ways to monetize our resources." The xfl was just one of the more audacious examples. Sam Muchnick helped promote the last world heavyweight championship boxing match in St. Louis — Joe Louis vs. Tony Musto, 1941 — and in later years served as the Harlem Globetrotters' local sub-agent; but his business was maximizing fannies in the seats at twice-monthly wrestling shows, period. Even his folio newsletter, mailed to subscribers and hawked at the arena, was at best a break-even proposition.

St. Louis Wrestling Club events were promoted via *Wrestling at the Chase* on kplr-tv, Channel 11, whose first announcer was Joe Garagiola (before he left to become host of the nbc *Today* show) and whose original venue was the ornately chandeliered Khorassan Room of the exclusive Chase-Park Plaza Hotel. Businessmen in suits and their wives in evening dresses tried not to spill wine on the tablecloths while they watched Dick the Bruiser use his Atomic Drop on Pat O'Connor. The formula was tight and, by wrestling standards, dignified: perhaps one Texas Death Match per year, a couple of masked men per decade, a finish involving a referee "bump" once in a blue moon. German and Japanese bad guys marked the xenophobic limit. Extracurricular tv skits, known as "angles," were eschewed. "Juice," or blood, was virtually nonexistent. Somewhere in the course of the season Sam would mix in a midget tag match and a women's special attraction.

Vince McMahon picks gleefully at race-baiting or any other market-tested social scab (recently the latent tension between wrestling's homophobia and homoeroticism has become explicit). Sam Muchnick's racism was more genteel, but of course it also had the effect of stifling opportunity. St. Louis remained a de facto Jim Crow town long after the 1954 Supreme Court decision, and Sam knew nothing if not how to get along. In the mid-sixties he finally brought in his first black wrestler, football star Ernie (The Cat) Ladd, and the African Americans from the North Side popped huge for him. Perhaps unsettled by the possibilities, Sam

Ernie "The Cat" Ladd administers his trademark thumb to the throat

kept Ladd buried in the undercards. (Ladd would go on to become one of the highest-profile black supporters of the presidential candidacy of George W. Bush.) It would be several more years before a black wrestler actually got a championship shot in St. Louis — and that would be a far inferior performer, Rufus R. Jones, whose hard head and soft belly conformed to the conventional view of a black male cartoon character.

There are other instructive contrasts between McMahon and Muchnick — notably the way the former places himself at the center of his on-camera cast, and even pushes his son Shane and daughter Stephanie into television stardom. Like the Godfather, Sam Muchnick preferred to shield his family.

His was a modest milieu bounded by sports-world cronies and local cops and pols. He spread a few nickels around, making sure that the state athletic commission was stocked with friendly faces and that the Friday night match results ran in the Saturday morning *St. Louis Globe-Democrat* (but little more — the best PR can be the kind that keeps your name *out of* the newspapers).

Sam Muchnick's St. Louis farewell – January 1, 1982: with Gene Kiniski, Joe Garagiola and Larry Matysik

Through such minimalism he cultivated a nice-guy image. Few doubted, however, that someone could survive so long in such a seedy business without a certain knack for intimidation. An otherwise unremarkable dresser, Sam always sported a sinister black homburg which, *St. Louis Post-Dispatch* sports editor Bob Broeg liked to joke, gave him "the appearance of a member of the Soviet secret police."

Sam's last show was on New Year's Day 1982. Later the same year, Vince bought Capital Wrestling Corporation, the company controlling the Northeast territory, which was owned by his father, Vincent J. McMahon, and his partners Gorilla Monsoon, Phil Zacko, and Arnold Skaaland. In 1963 the senior McMahon's group, which then included Toots Mondt and Willie Gilzenberg, had broken off from Sam's National Wrestling Alliance, started something called the World Wide Wrestling Federation, and crowned its own New York–based "world champion," Bruno Sammartino. But by the seventies there was again peace between the NWA and the folks of what had now been shortened to the World Wrestling Federation (WWF). On the East Coast they were even allowed to continue billing their guy as *the* champion. Wrestling promoters are smart enough to know that title changes are like election results: if they're not reported on TV they never happened.

But now it was a new world, a world of cable and deregulation, of snarky young promoters and multimedia marketing. Even junk culture had become something to be branded instead of closeted. Old-style wrestling was dead. The king was a high-low concept called "sports entertainment," and Vince McMahon was its pioneer and foremost practitioner. Simultaneously and magically, sports entertainment moves the carnival into the mainstream, infects the latter with the values of the former, and packages the merchandise to prove it.

Capital investment had been transformed since the night Lou Thesz escaped Fritz Von Erich's Iron Claw hours after the Kennedy assassination. So had the human stakes. In October 1997, WWF wrestler Brian Pillman was found dead in Minnesota of a heart attack — almost certainly brought on by his use of steroids, human growth hormone, and painkillers — just hours before the start of the *Badd Blood* pay-per-view from the new Kiel Center in St. Louis. Pillman had been scheduled for matches on the show against Dude Love and Goldust. McMahon taped a cut-in explaining the circumstances and ordered the show to go on. The next night, McMahon ran a tribute to Pillman, which included an appearance by his tearful widow, on *Raw*, the flagship USA cable network wrestling show.

In May 1999, WWF wrestler Owen Hart was killed when a high-wire stunt went awry shortly after the start of the *Over the Edge* pay-per-view from the Kemper Arena in Kansas City. McMahon ordered the show to go on. The next night he turned *Raw* into a tribute to Hart. That night's edition of *Raw* emanated from the Kiel Center in St. Louis.

In between, on December 30, 1998, Sam Muchnick died at age ninety-three. The funeral was held three days later at the chapel of Memorial Park Cemetery in suburban St. Louis. Probably the only figure in attendance even remotely recognizable to contemporary wrestling fans was the legendary former NWA champion, 81-year-old Lou Thesz, who arrived late after cracking up his car while driving straight through on ice-slick roads from his home in Virginia. Sitting alongside my father, my sister, and my cousins, I could make out people like Moose Mueller, the off-duty cop who used to moonlight as a *Wrestling at the Chase* security guard. I felt like I was trapped on the set of the Woody Allen movie *Broadway Danny Rose.*

On Sam's instructions the funeral was co-officiated by a rabbi and Monsignor Meyer. In his eulogy, the priest tenderly remembered the evening thirty-five years earlier when he was summoned to deliver a prayer before wrestling fans grieving for their assassinated president. He remarked on how classy it all was.

"Who besides Sam Muchnick," Monsignor Meyer asked rhetorically, "would have thought of something like that?"

OK, enough Muchnick family history. On with the show. As both Sam and Vince would have agreed, it's the American way.

On with the show

CHAPTER 2

BORN-AGAIN BASHING WITH THE VON ERICHS

A Cute Concept Decays into a Macabre Body Count

The following is adapted from a story that would be selected for the anthology *Best Magazine Articles: 1988*.

The publication of the piece was something of a departure for mainstream journalism – even if, as Fritz Von Erich complained in a preemptive and more positive profile in *D* magazine, my investigation did appear in "a damn pornographic magazine!" Among other things, I was invited to appear on the *Late Show*, a short-lived competitor to Johnny Carson on the then-fledgling Fox network. The producer's preparation consisted of urging me to "blow the lid off wrestling," unencumbered, in all likelihood, by the reading of my article. The clueless host, Ross Shafer (a game-show emcee who was hired to pick up the pieces of the *Late Show* after Joan Rivers was fired), read similar verbiage off a cue card while introducing me. On the bright side, I got the chance to chat in the green room with another guest that night, the distinguished movie director Paul Mazursky.

A pre-publication story about the article in the *Dallas Times*

Percy Pringle with The Missing Link

Herald naturally led the wrestlers in World Class Championship Wrestling to ask their bosses, Fritz Von Erich and Ken Mantell, about it. The boys were told not to worry, that the family's vast influence had succeeded in getting the story killed. Soon one of the wrestlers discovered otherwise when he picked up the October 1988 issue of *Penthouse* from a convenience store rack, and it was promptly passed around the back seat of the car between spot shows throughout northern and eastern Texas. Someone once said it's a bad sign when you lie with full knowledge that you're going to get caught.

Later, Percy Pringle, the circuit's lead heel manager, left World Class to become a new character in New York: Paul Bearer, manager of The Undertaker. Pringle wrote in his resignation letter to Fritz Von Erich, "When I read the *Penthouse* article I knew the dream was over."

MAY 11, 1987. *Less than a month after his brother Mike killed himself because he felt he couldn't live up to the family name, Kevin Von Erich was working the main event in Fort Worth when something rare happened: a moment of spontaneous, unmediated terror. As the television cameras rolled, teenage girls squealed, and spectators shouted for blood, Kevin and his opponent crisscrossed off the ropes. No doubt they were setting up the usual wild finish — perhaps a variation on the patented Von Erich Iron Claw, or a violent collision followed by an out-of-control brawl outside the ring, or maybe a miscarriage of justice, with the ref taking an accidental bump and failing to see the heel clobber the babyface with a foreign object.*

We'll never know what the climax of this match was supposed to bring. For suddenly, without being touched, Kevin Von Erich's abused body defied the script. Instead of snapping smartly off the ring's taut ropes, he sagged heavily against the strands. Recoiling, he staggered toward the center of the canvas, then collapsed, torso convulsing, pupils rolled heavenward.

The fans in attendance at the Will Rogers Coliseum probably thought they were witnessing the first documented case of a professional wrestler falling into holy rapture. What they were actually seeing, though, was the champion of the World Class Wrestling Association simply passing out in the middle of the ring in the middle of a match.

No matter what those in legit sports and others of respectable breeding may think, wrestling is a subtle, extemporaneous art form; experienced pros pride themselves on their ability to salvage even the most sour finish. But Kevin Von Erich's swan dive supplied more grim reality than any ordinary eight-man tag-team match could bear.

Chaos reigned at ringside. The bell rang. The TV cameras were switched off. Wrestler Tommy Rogers scrambled through the ropes and performed CPR on his fallen partner, who was turning blue.

Later, after being released from Harris Methodist Hospital in Fort Worth, Kevin explained on television how he'd nearly been killed by a dreaded new oriental neck punch, courtesy of his hated rival Brian Adias. Kevin vowed to avenge the blow the next time they met, whether it be in Fort Worth or Dallas or Mesquite or Lubbock or . . .

Thus, with the heady brew of half-truth and chutzpah that only the hypemeisters of wrestling could concoct, a genuine brush with mortality became just another angle to sell tickets.

If you've been living anywhere north of the Seychelles Islands, you already know the pro wrestling "resurgence" is the marketing phenomenon of the eighties. If you're a fan of any seriousness, you've also heard of the Von Erichs, wrestling's tragedy-plagued, all-American first family. Hard-core aficionados will tell you that long before Madison Avenue turned Hulk Hogan, Rowdy Roddy Piper, and Andre the Giant into household names, the hottest promotion in the country wasn't run by New York's World Wrestling Federation, but by Dallas's World Class Championship Wrestling.

The furor over World Class centers on the fuhrer of World Class: Jack B. Adkisson on his driver's license, Fritz Von Erich to you and me — a Prussian bad guy who, through the magic of media manipulation, transmogrified into a god-fearing crowd favorite before retiring as an active wrestler. As a full-time promoter, Von Erich proceeded to build an empire around his photogenic sons: David, the rambunctious Yellow Rose of Texas; Kerry, the dumb but lovable jock with the long thick hair and Conan pecs; Kevin, the barefooted high-flying specialist; and Mike, the earnest overachiever. Together they pioneered the use of modern rock-video production techniques for their televised wrestling shows and shattered attendance records in the early 1980s.

Today the Von Erich dynasty is in ruins, both personally and professionally — a cautionary tale of the bitter price of celebrity, the excesses of parental authority, and the dangers in believing

Eddie Smith raises David Von Erich's hand, with his father, the inventor of the Iron Claw, by his side, September 21, 1980

your own press clippings. Two of Fritz's boys suffered drug-related deaths. A third continues to wrestle despite a crippling leg injury. The fourth and oldest, Kevin, is the hapless heartthrob who took that unscheduled pratfall in Fort Worth. At a show at Reunion Arena last Christmas, shortly after selling a share of the promotion to a new partner, Fritz pulled his latest stunt to drum up sympathy for himself and his kids: he faked a seizure that, for a while, allegedly, left him near death.

Somewhere along the way a cute concept decayed into a macabre body count.

"I've been around a lot of special athletes, but I've never witnessed anything like the development of this single family that, in its day, completely conquered the world of wrestling," says Bill Mercer, a Dallas sportscaster who used to announce for the Von Erichs. "For one son to follow in his father's footsteps is common enough. For two sons to do so is extraordinary. That a man could wield enough family control for three and four sons . . . well, it's all pretty amazing. And also pretty scary."

Indeed, in the figure of patriarch Fritz Von Erich, this ten-gallon tragedy, rife with Texas-size scandal, becomes a melodrama of Shakespearean proportion. In addition to being one of the top powerbrokers in wrestling — that bizarre amalgam of sport and theater rooted in the nineteenth-century carnival tent — Fritz is a born-again Christian, a respected member of the nation's largest Southern Baptist congregation, a pillar of the community with ties to everyone from former presidential candidate Pat Robertson to Forbes 400 oilman H.R. "Bum" Bright, owner of the Dallas Cowboys. In those capacities Fritz airbrushes his sons' image, exploiting not only their bodies but also their misfortunes. The fall of the house of Von Erich is Jim and Tammy Faye Bakker with a dropkick, a combination of pseudo-athletic zeal and quasi-religious righteousness, a farcical footnote to the sleazy legacy of televangelism.

There's one key difference, though.

At the PTL ministry, home of Jim and Tammy Faye, the leitmotiv was sexual and financial impropriety; the scars were essentially psychological and fiduciary.

At World Class Championship Wrestling, people are dying.

MAY 6, 1984. *Wrestling history was made as 32,123 fans at Texas Stadium — plus other thousands via closed-circuit television — attended the David Von Erich Memorial Parade of Champions. In those pre-*WrestleMania *days, the $402,000 gate was the second-largest of all time.*

The atmosphere was much like it had been at David's funeral three months earlier at the First Baptist Church in Denton. On that occasion almost 3,000 admirers — many of them kids listening to the service on a makeshift public-address system on the church lawn — paid their respects. You couldn't buy a yellow rose in north Texas that day. Now his fans were waiting in the longest concession lines this side of a Prince concert to pay $10 for the same eight-by-ten color photo of David that used to go for $3. Underscoring the rock-show mood was fan Glen Goza's performance of his eulogy in song, "Heaven Needed a Champion," which had been getting airplay on Dallas radio stations.

The main event, between Kerry Von Erich and Ric Flair for the world title, had great "heat," literally and figuratively. After thirteen minutes Kerry pinned Flair with a backslide; the championship that had been promised to his late brother was his. As the gold belt was presented to Kerry, who was surrounded by family and friends, tears flowed unashamedly under the searing Texas sun.

The Von Erichs refused to grant an interview for this story. "We see no reason to respond," Fritz wrote in a certified letter, because this article "is not based on fact and appears to be of malicious intent."

A recent cover story in *D*, a Dallas magazine, describes Fritz bellowing to a business associate not to tell us a thing: "We're not going to be written about like trash. . . . My family isn't going to be in a damn pornographic magazine!"

As we were going to press, Fritz's partner, Ken Mantell, told the *Dallas Times Herald* that "anyone who says the Von Erichs are not a Christian family, well, that's a crock. An outright lie. . . . Being a Christian does not mean you are perfect, does not mean you haven't made mistakes in your life. There's another book that says, 'Let he who is without sin cast the first stone.'"

A spokesman warned that the family was prepared to take legal action if any nuggets of official mythology, such as the circumstances of David Von Erich's death, were challenged. "His sons' image is very important to Mr. Von Erich, and he'll do what he feels is necessary in order to protect it," the spokesman said.

That much is certainly true, according to friends and foes alike in the ultra-secretive wrestling business.

"If you know Fritz," says a fellow promoter, Bill Watts, "you know he's sincere from the way he thinks. He truly believes the tragedies of his family have brought many, many youngsters to Christ. He thinks the Von Erichs are the most name-conscious family in sports."

Another promoter, Paul Boesch, agrees, but adds, "You have to wonder why, after all he's been through, he doesn't just find his

"Cowboy" Bill Watts ties up his masked foe

kids a nice hamburger stand somewhere and say, 'Here, you'll live longer this way.'"

Living longer, or shorter, was a tragic pattern established early in the marriage of Jack and Doris Adkisson. Their first son, Jack Jr., died in 1959, at the age of six, when he accidentally electrocuted himself outside in a rainstorm and drowned in a puddle. In those days, climbing the wrestling ladder, Fritz Von Erich was on the road constantly, working not only big-city arenas but also hundreds of tank towns in between.

Five more boys followed for the Adkissons, and by the time they were in their formative years Von Erich had bought out Dallas promoter Ed McLemore. Fritz also was a millionaire, largely through real estate investments in the Dallas–Fort Worth Metroplex during a couple of building booms in the 1970s. At one point he owned three airplanes, a cattle herd, and 5,000 quail. The family homestead was a 168-acre ranch near Lake Dallas (now called Lewisville Lake) in the town of Corinth, a small community in Denton County, north of Dallas, where Fritz served as a city councilman.

Two factors peculiar to the Dallas corporate culture contributed to Von Erich's business success. The first was the mystique surrounding his tenure as a football player at Southern Methodist University. In fact, Fritz was only a part-time offensive guard for one season at SMU in 1949 before leaving in a dispute with the coaches. But he managed to parlay those ninety-two minutes of blocking in front of the legendary Doak Walker — as well as a record discus throw in a track meet the following spring — into a niche in the SMU business clique. Dallas insiders describe this as a circle of powerful friends, including insurance magnates, bankers, and politicians, that controls much of the city's commercial life.

Then there was religion. In their book *The Von Erichs: A Family Album* — recently issued by Taylor Publishing, which specializes in Christian subjects — Fritz recalls being deeply moved by a sermon given by Dr. W. A. Criswell at the First Baptist Church in downtown Dallas around 1974. Shortly thereafter a divine voice guided Fritz to open his bible to Psalms 23. Not long after *that* the same powerful force compelled him to pull his car over to the shoulder of Interstate 35E one day and ponder his sins. Jack "Fritz Von Erich" Adkisson was born again.

The potent alchemy of sports, showbiz, and evangelism became explicit in the fall of 1981, when World Class Championship Wrestling began its relationship with the Christian Broadcasting Network's Dallas station, KXTX, Channel 39. A KXTX producer masterminded a new-style wrestling show that was briskly paced and employed four cameras, instant replays, and features edited to the beat of hit songs, à la MTV. In almost every respect the program's slick production values foreshadowed the manufacturing of "Hulkamania" on the East Coast three years later. At its peak World Class was syndicated into more than sixty markets across the country. (Starting in 1986 it also was seen regularly on ESPN, the cable sports network.) Fritz Von Erich even appeared several times on Pat Robertson's CBN talk show, *The 700 Club*.

Sons Kevin, David, and Kerry fit naturally into the core of the World Class talent stable — clean-cut, carefree country boys who looked good in the ring and even better on posters. "These boys were raised to be jocks," Fritz told *The Dallas Morning News* in 1983. "When they were youngsters, there were no kids scrawnier than mine. They were made into champions."

A close observer describes his paternalistic style as "hands-on": "Fritz is a very aggressive, physical guy. When you saw him with the boys, there was always a lot of hugging and displays of raw affection. But he was also very strict. It was all 'Yes, sir' and 'No, sir.' He ruled the roost with an iron hand."

Kevin started at fullback as a freshman at North Texas State University before a knee injury ended his football career. Kerry earned a track scholarship at the University of Houston by winning the state high school championship in the discus throw. Once they got into wrestling, though, David outshone both of them, due mostly to his fiercely independent spirit. As the boys grew older and married, Fritz continued to keep them on a short

Kerry Von Erich battles Fabulous Freebird Terry Gordy

chain — for years, all of their families lived within a mile or so of their parents. But in 1981 David rebelled. After an argument with his father, David went on the road. During nine months as a villain on the Florida circuit, he learned all the psychological tricks of the wrestling trade — working the crowd, calling the "spots" in a tough match, doing kick-ass interviews — with a thoroughness that would never have been possible if he hadn't had the courage to leave Fritz's glowering shadow. When David came back to Texas in late 1982, he was as polished and professional as the Beatles upon their return to Liverpool from Hamburg.

Thanks to David's smarts, Kerry's popularity, and their antagonists, the perfidious Fabulous Freebirds, Dallas grew into a major wrestling capital. In 1984 David was slated to capture the championship of the National Wrestling Alliance (one of the sport's several major bodies). In February of that year, hoping to season himself further and enhance his recognition abroad, he embarked on his second tour of Japan.

His first scheduled match, in Tokyo, never happened. The same day, David was found dead on the floor of his hotel room. He was twenty-five years old.

The cause, or causes, of David's death are a mystery. The Von Erichs say he died of a ruptured intestine caused by a hard lick during a match in Japan. That's obviously false, since David hadn't yet wrestled there. Nor can we put much stock in the family's other kaleidoscopic accounts, which have included but are not limited to (a) a stroke, (b) a heart attack after a strenuous match, and (c) food poisoning from eating sushi.

Inside dressing rooms and booking offices the gospel has always been that David died of drugs. Sources close to the handful of American personnel who accompanied him on that tour — who included fellow wrestling star Bruiser Brody — confirm that in the hours following the discovery of his body by a Japanese wrestling official and before the arrival of the police, drugs were flushed down the toilet. There is even reason to wonder if an autopsy was performed before the body was flown back to the States. (The Von Erichs at first offered to show me a copy of David's autopsy report and death certificate, but later reneged.)

The drug hidden from the authorities was a sleeping medication called Placidyl. If David mixed it with alcohol (and he was known to be fond of Jack Daniels), he may well have taken a lethal dose and, in the isolation of a foreign hotel room, been beyond the reach of timely help. Of course it's also entirely possible that a drug reaction compounded the effects of a stomach disorder.

Whatever it was that did David in, his loss devastated World Class. Fritz's religious tone became more strident and sectarian than ever; the show now even featured an official World Class chaplain, a charismatic minister named Gary Holder, who regularly used airtime to sing his boss's praises. The other brothers' histrionics increasingly resembled those of just another old-fashioned local-family promotion with a flashy production number. Eventually Fritz lost interest in the day-to-day operations and retreated to his new house near Tyler. Weekly shows at the Sportatorium used to be automatic sellouts; now they were sometimes lucky to draw 200 people. The booking agenda lurched from the creation of a phony Von Erich "cousin" to the use of female mud wrestlers.

In 1987 World Class tried to turn things around by parting

company with KXTX and signing a new production deal with Bum Bright, whose personal fortune is estimated at more than $600 million. But by then Connecticut promoter Vince McMahon had already turned his World Wrestling Federation into a cash cow with unprecedented international multimedia merchandising.

David's demise shook the wrestling industry; it was one of those events, like JFK's assassination or Buddy Holly's plane crash, that utterly reshaped the landscape. Further, the hoopla surrounding David's funeral created the uneasy sense that this goofy fringe form of junk entertainment was getting too big for its britches, but at the same time no one was prepared to do anything about it. The money and glory were simply too good to resist. Virtually overnight, wrestling was repositioning itself near the mainstream of the sports and entertainment spectrum via the brave new world of video. This sea change brought both unforeseen marketing opportunities and unforeseen human costs, creating responsibilities many in this enterprise of excess couldn't handle.

Abuse of drugs, especially cocaine and steroids, had long been part of the game. Now the sums of disposable income grew larger, the pressure to beef up physiques more intense, the one-night stands more far-flung and demanding. During pro wrestling's renaissance, the deaths of athletes in their twenties and thirties — not to mention the auto accidents and legal scrapes stemming from their impairment — became almost as commonplace as packed houses and children's toy deals. And some of the most egregious examples emanated from that bastion of Christian virtue, World Class.

The most potentially damaging drug incident was Kerry's arrest at Dallas–Fort Worth International Airport in June 1983. Kerry and his wife were returning from their honeymoon in Puerto Vallarta, Mexico, when U.S. Customs agents, during a routine inspection, caught him with eighteen unmarked tablets in his right front pocket. Inside the crotch of his pants was a plastic bag containing an assortment of nearly 300 other pills (including codeine, diazapem, Librium, and possibly Percodan), ten grams of marijuana, and 6.5 grams of "blue and white powder." The Von Erichs wove the ensuing publicity into the World Class TV storyline, vaguely suggesting that Kerry had been framed by the Freebirds, their archrivals. Eighteen months later, after behind-the-scenes maneuvering, the charges were dropped by the Tarrant County district attorney.

With that kind of discipline from the top, the word quickly spread that World Class was one of the worst drug offices in wrestling — a reputation reinforced in February 1986 when Gino Hernandez, one of its leading stars, died of a massive cocaine overdose. Shortly before his death, Hernandez was feuding on TV with Chris Adams, and they had recently done one of those ridiculous skits in which the dastardly Hernandez supposedly blinded the gentlemanly Adams.

That gave World Class announcer Bill Mercer the opportunity to put everything in perspective. "We have suffered two terrible tragedies in the last week — the blinding of Chris Adams and the death of Gino Hernandez," Mercer deadpanned.

Dallas wrestling program: the "blinding" of Chris Adams

FEBRUARY 2, 1987. *Kerry Von Erich, on crutches, slipped undetected through the stage entrance of the Fort Worth Convention Center for his first match since June 1986, when he had suffered a dislocated hip, a crushed right ankle, and internal injuries in a motorcycle accident.*

The fans had been assured that Kerry was ready to rumble. What they didn't know was that in the days following the accident — in which Kerry, traveling at an unsafe speed and making an ill-advised pass, plowed into the back of a patrol car — doctors almost had to amputate his foot. In thirteen hours of delicate microsurgery, they transplanted tissue from other parts of Kerry's body to his extremity in an effort to restore circulation and movement.

His opponent this evening was carefully instructed to "sell" for Kerry, for it was clear in advance that the man who was once among the most agile 250-pounders in wrestling would be virtually immobile. Still, they had to try to make a good show of it, so while Kerry changed into his trunks, a doctor filled a syringe with enough novocaine to numb Secretariat's hoof. Thus fortified, Kerry discarded his crutches, gritted his teeth, and hobbled into the ring. The match lasted five minutes and, as planned, Kerry won.

Afterward, when the novocaine wore off, an examination revealed that the ankle had rebroken. Four months later, in another operation, the foot was permanently fused into a walking position. On Thanksgiving in 1987 Kerry returned again, but he would never be the same.

One of the supreme ironies of World Class Championship Wrestling was that, through satellite technology, it became one of the most popular English-language programs in, of all places, Israel. It was on an August 1985 tour there that Mike Von Erich began the final fall of his short, tragic life.

If David's death was a pharmacological fluke, and Gino Hernandez's just an inevitable part of the business's ruthless fall-out, Mike's was a crime against decency. He never should have been a wrestler in the first place. Wrestling experts say that, with the possible exception of an occasional gimmick headliner such as Mr. T, Mike Von Erich was the single most pathetic piece of talent ever given a major push: small, tentative, and uncoordinated inside the squared circle, weak and halting in interviews, he had nothing going for him except his name.

Mike himself seemed to realize as much, and the guilt showed in his shifting eyes and erratic body language. Meanwhile, meeting his father's rigid expectations took an incalculable toll on his personal growth. Desperate to be as big as his brothers (he was billed as 220 pounds, but never weighed more than around 180), he took dangerous doses of steroids. Despondent over what he interpreted as his inability to live up to the family name, he took uppers and downers. Once shy and naturally likable, he became unruly and troublesome. At the end he made repeated cries for help — vague smoke signals at first, then stark sandwich-board signs, and finally wanton binges of self-destruction.

"I know we're only 'rasslers,' but we're still people and we have to treat our children like people," says Lou Thesz, arguably the sport's greatest performer from the 1940s through the mid-60s. "And you can't live your life through your kids. Fritz never understood that. I remember watching him one time backstage in Fort Worth. They had the TV monitor on, and there was this man — grossly overweight, chain-smoking — sitting there transfixed, watching his kids. Every time one of them did something, he'd turn and point to the screen and say, 'Isn't that great?' It was embarrassing."

In the Von Erich hagiography Mike was another great one, second only to Kevin in natural prowess. "He had a bad shoulder which stayed injured much of the time in high school," the *Family Album* states. "In track he was an All-District hurdler, long jumper, and discus thrower."

The memory of Lloyd Taliaferro, the athletic director at Lake Dallas High School, varies slightly. "Mike was a good boy, but he didn't compete much beyond the junior-varsity level," Taliaferro says. "Once, when he was a sophomore, he took a spill over a hurdle and hurt himself. That shook him up real bad."

Kevin, David, and Kerry at least had brief collegiate careers; Mike was funneled directly into wrestling. Within months he had a world-title shot. But despite Fritz's efforts to sell Mike as a stud, the fans never bought it. His frustration over his chronic bad shoulder and inability to get himself "over" manifested itself in sprees of ill-tempered violence outside the ring. In May 1985 Mike was charged with two counts of misdemeanor assault against Dr. Timothy Shepherd during an emergency-room altercation at First Texas Medical Center in Lewisville. A Denton County judge later acquitted Mike.

At Tel Aviv Stadium a bad bump in a rock-hard ring caused Mike's bum shoulder to pop out again. Following an operation on the shoulder performed as soon as he returned to Texas, he somehow contracted one of the rare male cases of toxic shock syndrome, a form of blood poisoning most commonly associated with tampon use.

Transferred to Baylor University Medical Center with a 105-degree fever, his kidneys next to useless, Mike clung to life as calls from concerned fans flooded the hospital switchboard. (The Von Erichs, with characteristic modesty, say the outpouring exceeded that which accompanied President Kennedy's trip to the Parkland Hospital emergency room in 1963.) The Von Erichs held a press conference to thank fans for their prayers. "Folks, let me tell you, a miracle took place, just that we have Mike today," Kevin said.

Fritz, however, was never content with just having his son alive. Even though Mike's weight dropped to 145 pounds, and many observers wondered if he'd suffered brain damage because of his slurred speech, Fritz lost no time repackaging him for the wrestling "marks." Mike was nicknamed "The Living Miracle" — fans were promised that he would defeat the odds, wrestle again, and claim a championship for God and family. To give the gimmick momentum, Mike was wheeled out in a car to wave to the 25,000 fans at the big October show at the Cotton Bowl. He made his official return to the ring on July 4, 1986. By then, he was also battling hepatitis.

"There's almost nothing about pro wrestling that really out-rages me, except for the Von Erichs," says Dave Meltzer, publisher of the *Wrestling Observer Newsletter*. In 1985 the publication named the exploitation of Mike's illness "the most disgusting promotional stunt" of the year.

The extent of Mike's physical and mental deterioration be-came apparent during the production of a TV special entitled *The Von Erich Trilogy*. At a taping session at a local health club, Mike was shown working out and getting himself back into fighting shape. The only problem was that after almost an hour of takes the crew still couldn't get a coherent interview out of Mike. Never one of the best "stick" men in wrestling, he was now hopelessly incompetent at the microphone. He fidgeted, complained about the heat, took his jacket off (revealing a stringy upper body), mentioned his wife (a no-no, for as a teen idol he was supposed to make the boppers believe he was eligible), and trailed off into a rambling monologue about the biblical character Hezekiah and his attending physician, Dr. William Sutker ("a great man who saved my life . . . He's Jewish, by the way, but he told me this has meant a lot to him spiritually and everything").

When the production crew finally gave up on the shoot, Mike retreated into the corner with a young friend, and the two of them bragged loudly about gang-banging a girl the night before.

The others at the gym turned away in revulsion. This wasn't wrestling. This wasn't religion. This was sickness.

Mike's weird behavior started leaking to the public.

- In November 1985 he totaled his Lincoln Continental when he ran off an embankment on State Highway 121 in Lewisville. Miraculously, he escaped with only a minor head injury.
- In May 1986 he was arrested in the early morning hours in Fort Worth and spent five hours in jail on charges of drunk and disorderly conduct.
- In February 1987 criminal mischief charges were dismissed

by a Tarrant County judge when Mike agreed to pay a
Fort Worth man $900 for kicking in the door of his car.

On April 11, 1987, Mike left a bar in Denton and was swerving
severely on Highway 377, headed toward his apartment in
Roanoke, when an officer pulled him over. Inside his Mercury
Grand Marquis were a small quantity of marijuana and two prescription bottles. One of them, with a dirty label more than three
months old, said it contained fifty tablets of Trinalin, an antihis-
tamine commonly prescribed for hay fever. The bottle actually
contained seventy-eight pills of five varieties: forty-two of a barbiturate; fifteen of a drug that wasn't analyzed but appeared to be
Tedral, an asthma medicine; ten of Buspar, an anxiety-relieving
agent; ten large, round reddish-orange pills that weren't identified; and one tablet of Darvocet, a painkiller.

Mike tried to bribe the cop. When that failed, he agreed to a
blood test. It showed a blood-alcohol content of .05 percent —
under the legal intoxication level of .10 percent but probably dangerous in combination with the other drugs in his system: 30
mg/L of ethchlorvynol (presumably from Placidyl, a cruel echo of
David's fate), 1.1 mg/L of butabital (a barbiturate), and 0.26 mg/L
of diazepam (indicating the intake of Valium or its equivalent).

The Von Erichs dispatched the family lawyer to the Denton
County jail to post Mike's $3,500 bond for drunk-driving and
controlled-substance charges. That was at 3:20 p.m. on Saturday,
and it was the last time anyone ever saw Michael Brett Adkisson
alive.

Early the next week a note was found in his apartment. It read:
"PLEASE UNDERSTAND I'M A FUCK-UP! I'M SORRY." Along the side
was scrawled: "I love U Kerry, Kevin & your families."

On Wednesday evening Mike's car was spotted near the entrance to a park on the south shore of Lewisville Lake. Inside was a
second note, which said simply, "Mom and Dad, I'm in a better
place. I'll be watching."

While police combed the many square miles of woods around

the lake, family members gathered for the vigil. But not Fritz — he went ahead with a scheduled evangelical crusade in Denton. That night in Lubbock, where Mike was scheduled to wrestle, the crowd was told that he was missing and that "foul play" was suspected. To the bitter end, Fritz Von Erich was determined to burnish the family image.

Hours later, a K-9 corps dog located Mike's body in a sleeping bag in a tangle of underbrush. The cause of death was acute Placidyl intoxication. He was twenty-three.

MAY 3, 1987. *The spring wrestling extravaganza at the home of the Dallas Cowboys was now an established tradition in the Metroplex sports scene. Of course, the latest death in the family dictated a few adjustments in the format. For one thing, instead of the Fourth Annual David Von Erich Memorial Parade of Champions, this was the David and Mike Von Erich Memorial Parade of Champions; for another, Sweet Brown Sugar had to substitute for Mike in the Canadian lumberjack match against Brian Adias.*

There were many other changes – most notably the presence of only 5,900 fans, who paid a mere $71,000. The Von Erichs had publicized a $100 ticket entitling the holder to a luxury box seat and a catered meal with the family. That idea was scrapped after only 14 fans signed up.

Between bouts gospel-singing prodigy Jill Floyd took to the ring to deliver a stirring reprise of "Heaven Needed a Champion." She was followed by the composer, Glen Goza, who recited a poem dedicated to young Mike.

And while Mike Von Erich's hallowed Christian memory was being invoked, maintenance workers prepared the pit for an upcoming women's mud-wrestling special attraction.

On September 12, 1991, a reporter for *The Fort Worth Star-Telegram* called me. "What is your comment on the suicide of Chris Von Erich?" he asked. I hadn't yet heard that Chris, at twenty-one the youngest surviving son of Jack and Doris Adkisson, had just fatally shot himself in the head. At only a few inches over five feet tall, Chris had been an even more ludicrous pro wrestling prospect than Mike – yet into the ring Chris, too, had gone. In my *Penthouse* article Chris was the unnamed "young friend" of Mike's who had joined him in loudly holding forth about double-teaming a girl.

Kerry Von Erich had drifted to the World Wrestling Federation, in the middle of cards, as "The Texas Tornado." The other wrestlers noticed that he never removed his right wrestler's boot, not even in the shower. During one match in Las Vegas the boot accidentally came off outside the ring for a few moments, and some of the spectators with close-up looks reported a gruesome sight. The strong suspicion is that Kerry wrestled much of the last seven years of his life on one foot, the right one having been amputated.

In 1992 the federal Drug Enforcement Administration got a tip that a wrestler on the WWF tour was traveling with a large supply of cocaine. In coordination with the local police, the DEA scheduled a raid of the dressing room prior to a WWF show at the St. Louis Arena. But someone in the building's management alerted the wrestling people and the raid came up empty. Besides, in the typical Keystone Kops style of drug warriors, the DEA apparently didn't realize that the subject of the original tip was Kerry Von Erich – and he had just gone off the wrestling tour and into drug rehab.

On Friday, February 20, 1993, Kerry, now back on the independent scene, was scheduled to wrestle the Angel of Death at the Dallas Sportatorium. But two days before that, Kerry, already on probation for a previous drug conviction, was indicted on cocaine possession charges.

On Thursday afternoon he went to his father's home in Denton County and said he wanted to drive around the property. Later in the day Fritz got worried and searched for his son. Kerry lay about a quarter of a mile away, dead from a self-inflicted .44-caliber bullet wound to the chest from a Smith & Wesson handgun. Kerry Adkisson was thirty-three.

On October 7, 2001, "Gentleman" Chris Adams, a mainstay of World Class Championship Wrestling in the eighties, was shot to death in a drunken brawl in Waxahachie. Three months earlier, Adams had been indicted for manslaughter in connection with the April 2000 death of his girlfriend from gamma hydroxybutyrate (GBH), the designer drug often used in "date rape."

In 2006, as this book was being prepared for press, a third-generation Von Erich, Ross — the son of Kevin and the nephew of David, Mike, Chris, and Kerry, and the grandson of Fritz (who died of cancer in 1997) — was in training to become a pro wrestler. Good grief.

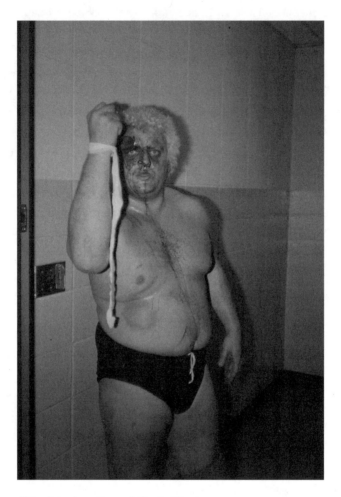

"The American Dream" Dusty Rhodes

CHAPTER 3

THE (THWAK!) DEREGULATION OF (THUMP!) PRO WRESTLING

The Bureaucrats Behind Hulk Hogan

This article was originally published in the June 1988 issue of *The Washington Monthly*. What I most remember about it – besides the Terry Gross *Fresh Air* interview – was the howling-with-laughter reaction to it from Rick Santorum, who called me. Santorum, then a young lawyer with Pittsburgh's Kirkpatrick & Lockhart, was working as a lobbyist for TitanSports, parent company of the then-WWF. He became the junior United States senator from Pennsylvania and nationally known for his reactionary views on abortion and gay rights. Santorum was defeated for reelection in November 2006.

Wahoo McDaniel's Indian Strap Match against Gorgeous Jimmy Garvin started out as just another day at the office. When he was supposed to bleed (or, as they say in the business, "juice"), Wahoo slipped a razor blade out from under his wrist band. Then, while Gorgeous Jimmy and his valet, Precious, distracted the crowd by arguing with the referee, Wahoo nicked a clump of scar tissue near his own scalp. His brow gushed copiously, and the 10,000 fans at Veterans Stadium popped with excitement.

Wahoo had juiced dozens, maybe even hundreds of times in his career, but never with such portentous consequences as at the *Great American Bash* in Philadelphia in July 1986. This time a piece of razor blade got lost in the gnarls of his scar tissue, where it stuck like a golf cleat to a wad of chewing gum. Wahoo, formerly a punishing linebacker in the old American Football League, worked the rest of the bout with the blade in his noggin. When he returned to the dressing room, the chairman of the Pennsylvania State Athletic Commission, James J. Binns, saw the mess at close range.

Binns ruled that there would be no more juice at the *Great American Bash*, or ever again in his jurisdiction. "Some of these guys have foreheads that look like raised atlas maps," Binns later told *The Philadelphia Inquirer.*

For Virgil Runnels — better known to wrestling fans as Dusty Rhodes, the American Dream — the commissioner's edict was worse than a whack with archrival Ric Flair's gold championship belt. Rhodes is chief booker for the National Wrestling Alliance. The World Wrestling Federation may sell itself as family entertainment, but Dusty's minions appeal to a harder core.

Infuriated by Binns, Dusty Rhodes nevertheless took a back seat to his tag-team partners: the lawyers. Eighteen months later, after intense lobbying by the industry and a critical report by an audit committee of the state legislature, the American Dream won. The Pennsylvania House of Representatives voted to put the athletic commission in a permanent sleeperhold, thereby removing any bureaucratic impediments to razor blades. The state senate is expected to follow suit. Commissioner Binns has resigned.

Pennsylvania thus seems poised to join Connecticut and Delaware as states that have deregulated wrestling in the past five years, and has swelled to nineteen the ranks of the states in which the sport is unsupervised. Of course, in some states that might be an improvement. As wrestling spins and kicks its way into a $300-

million-a-year business, state governments have created a bizarre regulatory maze that omits the rules most needed and erects ones where none are needed at all. But when it's the industry versus the regulators, it's usually the regulators that go down for the count.

HOW THEY DID IT: BARTER SYNDICATION

The New York Times, Op-Ed Page, January 18, 1986

While the Federal Communications Commission turns a blind eye, we are rapidly approaching the day when the majority of programs on local independent television stations will be directed by corporate advertisers.

The culprit is a new wrinkle called "barter syndication." At a conference of television program executives that runs through next week, this innovation will be the favorite toy of assorted game-show moguls, wrestling promoters, and producers of the hottest formats in "infotainment."

But it's time for someone to point out that barters are dangerous. They subvert the intent of communications law, add yet another layer of commercialism to broadcasting decisions, and undermine the balance of power in American television.

The hegemony of the three major networks is being broken, with cable and home video technologies accounting for much of this erosion. But where the viewers are going, to a large extent, is to the independents, and barter syndication is at the heart of their new clout.

Here's how it works. In the past, all but bottom-of-the-barrel syndicated shows were bought by local independent stations for cash. But in the anti-regulatory climate favored by the FCC, stations have begun paying packagers not with money but by yielding a portion of their commercial time. The packagers, having accumulated "barter" time in markets across the country, in turn broker it to national advertisers.

The seductiveness of barter packaging is based on its ability to give something to everyone. The stations get lower costs. Moreover, they get the presence of prominent national advertisers, which often forms a psychological tide that raises prices on local spots even when ratings don't improve. The national advertisers get another alternative to the networks. Finally, the syndicators get to create unofficial, sponsor-subsidized mini-networks. This technique is now used for many top shows, including *Wheel of Fortune*, *Entertainment Tonight*, *Solid Gold*, and *Lifestyles of the Rich and Famous*.

Perhaps the most vivid example of the handiwork of barters has been the so-called resurgence in professional wrestling. For years, wrestling on independent stations had been consistently, though quietly, outdrawing such network programs as Saturday morning cartoons and *Saturday Night Live*. But the popularity of the sport did not change our viewing habits until a handful of wealthy promoters – backed by toy manufacturers and other sponsors – seized on barter packaging to network their shows on independent stations across the country. Now we have round-the-clock wrestling on weekends.

The FCC refuses to investigate the growing practice of barters, contending that they are private arrangements between licensees and their clients. What's worse, the commission recently ended all limits on the number of commercial minutes per hour of program. Now stations don't even have to calculate a tradeoff between the national barter time they give away and the local advertising inventory they could have sold; they can simply cut the body of the program, add a few minutes of commercials, and profit at both ends.

There's nothing wrong with profits or with junk entertainment, which is both the glory and the folly of our egalitarian culture. But barter has turned the commercial broadcasting process on its head. Rather than buying programming, attracting an audience based on its quality, and then selling advertising based on that audience, television stations are shopping around to see which barter packagers offer the most up front. Instead of paying attention to their primary market of viewers, stations are serving a shadowy secondary market of unaccountable producers.

Recently we have seen the introduction in children's programming of advertising schemes that allow producers, broadcasters, and sponsors to share profits. Consumer advocates have expressed alarm over such blatant commercialization of programs directed at children. But these profit-sharing deals are nothing more than the natural extension of barters. Their proliferation may become one of the definitive legacies of communications policy in the Reagan era.

You're probably wondering if pro wrestling is a legitimate competition. No, Virginia, it is not. Its action, though dangerous and often surprisingly spontaneous, is choreographed. The matches themselves are a kind of brutal ballet in which the performers improvise the "spots" to create the illusion of violent combat until the scripted finish. Promoters call the shots, usually through backstage agents, who decide who gets pushed and generally ensure that the feuds circulate with all the freshness of *Dallas* subplots.

The first pro wrestling exhibitions in America were run out of carnival tents in the nineteenth century. The sport spread to the cities in the 1920s, becoming a sensation on television in the late forties and fifties with shows like *All-Star Wrestling* on the old DuMont network.

Even then, regulators were having trouble keeping the sport under control. Fortunately riots haven't been a serious problem in New York since Antonino Rocca sparked a brawl at the old

A rare photo of Antonino Rocca in the crowd at Madison Square Garden during the infamous 1957 riot

Madison Square Garden in 1957. An estimated 500 fans joined in that fray, which left two cops and several bystanders injured, and 200 chairs broken. Prodded by a vigilant commission, the chastened promoters thereafter instituted the practice of piping "The Star-Spangled Banner" over the public-address system at the conclusion of every controversial Rocca bout. While the partisans stood neutralized, security forces would spirit the bad guys out of harm's way.

One of those villains, Dick the Bruiser, got into so many fracases in New York State that, in his words, "I was suspended longer than the Brooklyn Bridge." Years later, when I asked the Bruiser how he managed to get himself reinstated, he winked and replied, "I called my mother." Dick the Bruiser's mother happened to be Indiana's Democratic National Committeewoman, Margaret Afflis Thompson.

Pro wrestling went into orbit in the brave new world of video. The current Barnum of Bounce is third-generation promoter

Vince McMahon, hypemeister and head of the Connecticut-based World Wrestling Federation. He looks like Alfalfa from *The Little Rascals* might have had he pumped iron. He's also a marketing genius. Today the WWF generates more of its revenue from such sources as pay-per-view cable television (where viewers dole out cash for each show), as well as videocassettes, kids' dolls, and T-shirts, than it does from live ticket sales. Since the company is privately held, it has not released its revenues. Its haul has been estimated at around $150 million a year.

In most states, boxing and wrestling have been lumped together in a peculiar regulatory scheme. The favored term, "athletic commission," overstates its purview. More accurate is the name of Washington, D.C.'s Boxing and Wrestling Commission (whose chairwoman Cora Wilds, incidentally, resigned last year after reports she was double-billing expenses). Across the country, commissions range from independent, governor-appointed supervisory panels to the cobwebbed corners of departments of state or labor or consumer affairs.

The commissions' promotion of safety standards for boxing is

Kimala and his "handler," Kimchee

heavily subsidized by rasslin'. In New York, for example, wrestling generated $302,262 in 1987 — almost three times as much as boxing. Even in California, where boxing events are staged more often than in any other state, wrestling revenues last year brought in more than double those of the sweet science ($271,806 to $122,292) through a 5 percent tax on gate receipts.

Beyond tax collection, the standard justification for wrestling regulation comes from people like Marvin Kohn, deputy commissioner of the New York State Athletic Commission. Kohn argues that promoters have always wanted a government superstructure because "we lend credibility to their product."

In New York State, credibility seethes from Part 225 of the athletic commission's rules. In Section 225.2 there's the concession that we're dealing with "exhibitions only." On the other hand, Section 225.11 asserts, that's no excuse for "unfair or foul tactics" such as "striking, scratching, gouging, butting, or unnecessarily punitive strangleholds." (Necessarily punitive strangleholds will always have their place.) Miscreants are cautioned that "unsportsmanlike or physically dangerous conduct or tactics" can result in disqualification. And let's not forget proper ring attire: fans of Kimala, the Ugandan Headhunter, and of Brutus (The Barber) Beefcake can sleep soundly knowing that the type and color of their trunks were approved by the commission, in accordance with Section 225.19.

The commission is charged with protecting the health and safety of participants, but doesn't neglect the financial protection of various hangers-on — such as Jose Torres, the $68,000-a-year chairman, ex-light-heavyweight boxing champ, and Norman Mailer's pre-Jack Abbott literary protégé. In New York no wrestling takes place without the presence of ring inspectors, who get $39 per event and are responsible, among other things, for making sure the corner turnbuckles are securely in place. Their service is greatly appreciated by George (The Animal) Steele, who as part of his act frequently lunches on the turnbuckles both during and after his bouts.

The Animal, a former Detroit high school teacher with a heart irregularity, is more leery of the official commission doctor, who checks the blood pressure of all wrestlers before they perform. A 1985 show at the Nassau Coliseum featured a steel-cage match between Captain Lou Albano, then 52 and grotesquely obese, and Classy Fred Blassie, the Hollywood Fashion Plate, then 69 and with an artificial hip that forced him to walk with the aid of a cane. Thanks to the attending physician, we have it on good authority that Albano's and Blassie's diastolic readings passed muster.

LET'S MAKE A DEAL

Mother Jones, June/July 1987

This year's conference of the National Association of Television Program Executives (NATPE) featured a bayou bash sponsored by Fox television stations, a band from the Wright Patterson Air Force Base courtesy of Lorimar Telepictures, and enough grog from Ted Turner to swab all quarter-of-a-million square feet of the New Orleans Convention Center floor. But the real attraction, as every year, was syndicated programming – the shows that don't appear on the three major networks but are distributed, one by one, to stations across the country. For five days station personnel and marketing specialists sampled the wares of more than 250 exhibitors, whose screening rooms and slick brochures showcased programs like *Secrets and Rumors* (in which celebrities reveal their own private peccadilloes and contestants get to determine who's telling the truth), and *T and T*, starring Mr. T as a private investigator.

For timid general managers and program directors with tight budgets, there was also the alternative of the shop-at-home television services that have exploited the current mania for deregulating the airwaves so shamelessly that even people within the industry are starting to feel threatened by the implications. The home-shopping craze formed the backdrop as more than 7,000 general managers, program directors, and marketing specialists flocked to New Orleans.

In the brave new world of video – with cable and satellite technology, VCR's in nearly half our homes, and new stations coming on the air at a breakneck clip – NATPE has become one of the primary nerve centers for the delivery of junk culture in America. It's both a real-life version of *Let's Make a Deal* and the apotheosis of the Reagan ethic, a never-never land where spectacle persists in subsuming substance, and where the barons of broadcasting wine, dine, and wallow in their own hype. NATPE may be the only place where you can find a legit marriage ceremony – a promo for an offering called *The Wedding Show* – drowned out by the cacophony of disco music and the bumping and grinding of a bevy of *Solid Gold* dancer imitators from a nearby booth. Only at NATPE does Dr. Ruth hold a symposium in which she asks average couples from Middle America, flown in to discuss life as Nielsen families, if the pressure of maintaining diaries of their viewing habits disrupts their sex lives.

While the convention's best food could be had at the cavernous exhibits of the old-line Hollywood studios, the most nouveau-riche excesses belonged to King World, the distributor of *Wheel of Fortune.* Other syndicators might settle for a simple refreshment stand and a full-service bar inside an eighty-by-fifty-foot cubicle of private offices and screening rooms; but Roger and Michael King opted for a space-age switchboard in the reception area, a striated glass dome reaching fifteen feet into the air, and a ring of cushy pews surrounding a fountain court strewn with hanging plants. Station executives lounged on the benches with their sandwiches and drinks as they waited in line to press Vanna White's flesh.

The tackiness of the King brothers epitomizes the transformation of NATPE, which used to be just another modest trade show whose prototypical figure was a lone frenetic salesman lugging an overstuffed briefcase. The move upscale began in the mid-1970s, when the Federal Communications Commission opened up the marketplace for independent producers by creating the so-called access period – the hour between the evening news and the prime-time slate, during which stations affiliated with NBC, CBS, or ABC were forbidden from using reruns of old network shows. Ideally the affiliates were supposed to use access to test innovative local programming; in practice, of course, most of them simply aired more game shows and infotainment schlock, and *Wheel of Fortune* became a national obsession.

The stakes of the game were raised in the era of galloping deregulation at the FCC under Reagan appointee Mark Fowler, a relentless free-market ideologue. In a sweeping 1984 order the commission rescinded all restrictions on both the number and the length of commercials. The locus of the business promptly shifted from old-fashioned program peddling to new-fangled deal making. Instead of selling their shows to stations for cash, syndicators now could barter them in exchange for more and more commercial minutes, then turn around and sell the time themselves to national sponsors. Some producers, such as wrestling promoters and toy manufacturers, went further by paying stations to get their shows on the air, or cutting the stations in on the profits generated by the sales of tickets to the wrestling matches or of the dolls featured on children's programs. Broadcasters were thus able to manipulate the process that, for all its tendency to reduce popular will to the lowest common denominator, had always been the premise of their enterprise: the burden of attracting an audience and selling advertising targeted at that audience.

A speculative market in broadcast licenses added to the hysteria for commercialization in 1982 after the FCC abolished the so-called anti-trafficking rule, which had required a new station owner to wait at least three years before reselling it. Licenses began to be traded as furiously as stock-index futures at the triple-witching hour. Two years later the commission also increased from seven to twelve the number of stations a single company could own, and entrepremergerism flourished.

But as NATPE '87 approached, the independent TV bubble was bursting. The advertising market had stagnated, crippling many of the more than 250 independent stations that had started up since 1976. A number of weak UHF outlets, underfinanced by junk bonds and operated by inept gold-rush prospectors, had gone belly-up — prodding the convention's organizers to include on the program a seminar on the vagaries of Chapter 11 bankruptcy. It was in the context of this crisis that home shopping fired the feeble imaginations of TV programmers.

For all his flaws as an agency head, Fowler is a phrasemaker of almost Maoist profundity; in his most quoted line he once defined a television set as "a toaster with pictures." Nothing makes the bottom line toastier than home shopping, which eliminates the unproductive nuisance of having to dole out some sort of information and entertainment to the public, gives the station a commission on the sale of every joy buzzer and dribble glass, and relieves the happy consumer of having to dash to the store and hunt for a parking space.

"We're more like magazines now," crowed Richard Robertson of Lorimar, which launched *ValueTelevision*, a daily one-hour shopping show, in conjunction with Rupert Murdoch's new Fox network. "We're able to get revenues both from advertisers and from viewers."

At the top of the list of companies determined to nail us coming and going was the upstart Home Shopping Network, last year's darling of Wall Street. Expanding from its base on cable, HSN adopted the crude but effective strategy of swallowing UHF stations; in a piece of legal legerdemain, it managed in some cases to buy the stations' assets without assuming their liabilities. Whether HSN — whose stock is now plummeting as precipitously as it rose — represents a fly-by-night fad or television's face of the future remains to be seen. All the syndicators at NATPE knew is that they were stuck overnight not only with broken contracts but also with a dwindling demand for straight entertainment. Naturally they screamed at the feds for relief. As in the airline industry, the speed with which deregulators become re-regulators can be breathtaking.

"The business has gotten out of control," complained Marvin M. Grieve, head of MG/Perin, a small syndication outfit, and president of the Association of Program Distributors. "The free marketplace is not being responsible. What happens if some used-car dealer in Peoria buys a station and sells cars on it twenty-four hours a day? How could a guy running for Congress ever buy a thirty-second spot?"

Grieve's concern for the enlightenment of the electorate was moving. In New Orleans the scantily clad vixens of one of his aggrieved properties, *Gorgeous Ladies of Wrestling*, cavorted inside a pink ring, arousing the purely professional interest of hordes of sweaty-palmed station executives and their less-amused spouses.

The fact that the line is being drawn in the sand at round-the-clock home shopping is an indication of how radically the FCC's Fowler has altered the terms of the debate. When he took over in 1981, citizens were scouring station logs, challenging commercial clutter, and demanding quotas for public-service programming. Today, with Fowler having returned to private life, we're arguing over whether *ValueTelevision* should be limited to one-hour blocks.

"The public's interest," Fowler once said, "will determine the public interest." But in an earlier era the practice of allowing producers to dangle cash in front of drooling licensees was called payola. Now it's called free enterprise. In one of the permanent triumphs of the Reagan revolution, the medium has been remade, top to bottom, in the Great Communicator's own fatuous image.

The Junkyard Dog

Other states set an equally inspiring example. In Maryland wrestling promoters must set aside two ringside rows at every show for commission officials. In Missouri the most heated issue is a ban against jumping off the top rope; to say the least, this prohibition cramps the style of Jimmy (Superfly) Snuka, the acrobatic Polynesian whose coup de grace consists of diving onto his supine victim. In Oregon they recently banned the blade; now when Portland fans clamor for blood, wrestlers simply do it "the hard way," grinding a knuckle into each other's foreheads or rubbing against ropes or ring posts.

In New Mexico the blood-pressure tests are always a hassle because of the high altitude and spicy Mexican food. The big, wasted black man who bills himself as The Junkyard Dog once flunked half a dozen times in Albuquerque before finally getting his pressure down to an acceptable level. The show was juggled so

JYD could go on later — making this the only known case of a wrestler's being switched from the undercard to the main event because of concerns over his health.

In Pennsylvania, the Byzantium of wrestling regulation, the buckets of red blood are matched by rolls of red tape. Long before the Wahoo McDaniel contretemps, the World Wrestling Federation complained about an official ringside commission table, which always had to be covered with a white tablecloth. The table's sharp corners threaten to cause far more injuries than the cushioned mats that WWF wrestlers collapse on when they're tossed outside the ring. But if the commission folds, as is expected, so might the table.

In 1972 an overeager commissioner named Joe Cimino ordered the strict enforcement of *all* amateur-style rules. At a Pittsburgh show his referee dutifully set about disqualifying wrestlers left and right for fake punches, hair-pulling, and use of the ropes; as a result, an hour's worth of scheduled matches lasted a mere twenty-two minutes. Since the show was being shot live for TV, this left thirty-eight minutes, but those watching at home got a treat: an unrehearsed, honest-to-God, on-camera shouting match between Cimino and wrestler Bruno Sammartino.

So when the Pennsylvania athletic commission came up for review last year under a 1981 sunset bill, the wrestling community was only too eager to air its complaints. As it turned out, however, some of the best dirt came from people within the commission itself. The audit committee learned of turf battles between the executive director, a full-time staff official, and the commissioners, who were paid on a per diem basis to attend meetings and events while trying to direct the day-to-day operations. Further blurring the flow charts was a confusing district system, which had different commissioners enforcing different guidelines in each section of the state.

The auditors didn't go so far as to recommend abolishing the commission — only cutting the number of deputies and trimming its authority. But once their report reached the legislature, the World Wrestling Federation's savvy lobbyists pulled the levers on the fate of the beleaguered agency as expertly as Macho Man Savage throws a flying elbow. At a September 1987 show in Hershey, they handed out complimentary tickets, hors d'oeuvres, beer, and soda to the chairman of the state house Government Committee and more than twenty staff members of the Governor's Office of Legislative Affairs and the Department of State. Three months later, the vote flattened the commission.

But it was the legislation's fine print that really rang the bell. Not only was the state wrestling tax reduced from 5 to 2 percent, but the surety bond for promoters was raised from $3,000 to $10,000. Dave Meltzer, publisher of the *Wrestling Observer*, an insider newsletter, notes that this last provision will have the effect of helping major promotions like the WWF and the NWA by shutting out smaller independent operators.

"In other words, as usual, Vince McMahon got exactly what he wanted," Meltzer concludes. You better believe it.

THE WAY IT BECAME

Shane McMahon gets in on the action

CHAPTER 4

SEX AND THE GRITTY

And You Thought Vince Was Joking When He Said He Wanted His Kids to Follow Him in the Family Business

In 2000 I was asked to write an article about sex and wrestling by my friend Jack Heidenry, editor of the soon-to-be-defunct online magazine *ThePosition.com*, which was published by the new Museum of Sex in New York. I would dearly love to deliver a deep, deep, double-underhook suplex to Daniel Gluck, the sleazebag who founded the museum and stiffed me out of my fee.

On a Monday night in the mid-1980s, following a World Wrestling Federation show at Madison Square Garden in New York City, a teenage member of the ring crew — the guys who set up and tear down the three-roped, four-posted, twelve-turn-buckled squared circle — was given a piece of fatherly advice by a veteran WWF performer.

The ring crew kid, whose name was Tom Cole, had been reviewing assignments for the next stop on the WWF circuit with his supervisor, Mel Phillips. When Phillips walked away, the wrestler standing next to Cole nudged him and said, "Watch yourself around Phillips. He's bad news." Prophetic words.

A few years later Phillips was a central figure in a pedophilia scandal that came within a federal grand jury of sinking the WWF, and Tom Cole was the chief whistleblower. More on that in a moment. In the institutional memory of the pro wrestling public, where the results of last month's pay-per-view event have already vaporized, the events of the early nineties may as well have taken place in Greco-Roman times.

The wrestler who made the remark to Cole had recently retired from the ring due to blood clots in his lung (a condition that can be caused by abuse of muscle-enhancing anabolic steroids, though he claimed it was from Agent Orange). His forced retirement turned out to be a big break, however, for he soon found fame as a heel commentator on WWF television. Now he was about to head to Hollywood for an even bigger break: a role alongside Arnold Schwarzenegger in the movie *Predator*. The

ex-wrestler signed his checks "James Janos." Aided by a state law allowing political candidates to use their *noms de guerre* on the ballot, he later would be elected mayor of Brooklyn Park, Minnesota, then governor of Minnesota.

He was, is, Jesse "The Body" Ventura.

The Governor of Minnesota: Jesse Ventura

You don't have to be a Reform Party renegade, a French semiotician, or a board member of the Parents Television Council to know that sex and wrestling go together like a horse and carriage.

In an earlier era they used to call this pseudo-sport "grunting and groaning." The pejorative was despised by my late uncle Sam Muchnick. "They do grunt and they do groan," he once conceded to me, "but putting it that way sounds so . . . *undignified*." Sam was perhaps the industry's most important promoter before wwf hypemeister Vince McMahon crossed new technology with postmodern perversity to create the strangest marketing juggernaut in pop-culture history.

Part of McMahon's particular genius was to cut out the middleman, end any pretense of dignity, and give the people exactly what they wanted: homophobia locked in mortal combat with homoeroticism. But this is not a disquisition on the sexual content of the wrestling product. It is a report on the companion phenomenon of sex *inside* wrestling. The question is whether the backstage manipulations of promoters, bookers, performers, and hangers-on mirror the displaced fetishes, dominance games, and double (and sometimes, single) entendres so boldly evident on the sunny side of the proscenium.

And the answer is: Uh, yeah.

Understand, for starters, that wrestling sex is to real sex what wrestling violence is to real violence. Just as the most effective punch is the pulled variety, the best fuck is the mind kind. Consenting adults trespass this blue line at their own risk. For proof we offer Kevin Sullivan, a booker, or storyline weaver, for Ted Turner's World Championship Wrestling, the wwf's chief rival.

Four years ago Sullivan was casting about for a way to put "heat" on Chris Benoit, a technically brilliant but relatively colorless Canadian wrestler, when Sullivan hit upon a brilliant idea. It involved Sullivan's wife Nancy Daus, a buxom brunette who appeared on wcw television as a valet known, economically, as

Kevin Sullivan and "Woman"

"Woman." Sullivan cooked up a subplot (an "angle" in carny patois) whereby Woman left Sullivan for Benoit.

Wrestlers tend to take method acting to extremes. In this instance, to give the gimmick credibility, Sullivan ordered his wife and Benoit to hang out together 24/7. When Chris went to the gym, Nancy went with him. When he went to his hotel room, she . . . well, you get the point. Before long, life was imitating art. On February 23, 2000, Nancy celebrated the birth of her baby boy, Daniel Christopher Benoit. It is not known if Sullivan sent a shower gift. Chris Benoit was by now in the WWF.

"Kevin Sullivan," says *Wrestling Observer Newsletter* publisher Dave Meltzer, "booked his own divorce."

Legendary wrestler Bret "Hitman" Hart saw his fourteen-year marriage to his wife Julie (not a TV character) collapse, in part under the strain of sexual innuendo, on a 1997 WWF tour ably captured in the award-winning documentary *Hitman Hart: Wrestling With Shadows*. In one memorable scene, Hart and his then-nemesis Shawn Michaels are recording a promotional

Missy Hyatt accompanies Eddie Gilbert

"shoot" for a series of upcoming matches. The two men were said to truly detest each other, and their insults, though elliptical to the uninitiated, added up to more than a contrived "work."

At one point Michaels says to Hart, "You've been having a lot of 'sunny' days lately" — a reference to Hart's rumored affair with wrestling personality Sunny (Tammy Sytch). Hart, who now wrestles for wcw, denies the rumor. It also must be noted that Hart has had more important things on his mind since the 1999 death of his brother, Owen, during a stunt at a wwf pay-per-view show.

Husband-and-wife combos are no less common among wrestlers than in other professions. Unions of recent vintage include Randy "Macho Man" Savage and The Lovely Elizabeth (they're now divorced). Eddie "Hot Stuff" Gilbert, who would die of a drug overdose, married and divorced both Missy Hyatt and Medusa Miceli. The aforementioned Ms. Sytch married wrestler Chris Candido. And there are many, many others.

The thinking person's wrestling fan, therefore, ponders the future of those volatile lovebirds Hunter Hearst Helmsley (Paul Levesque) and Stephanie McMahon.

That Stephanie is billed with a hyphenated surname on *SmackDown* is about as meaningful as the championship belt her bogus hubby once held and may one day regain. Still, how many opportunities does a man get to French-kiss the boss's daughter on national TV? Insiders describe the relationship as legitimately on-again, off-again, or at least serious enough to make Triple H forget his former squeeze, Chyna (Joanie Laurer), whose biceps measure somewhere between Stephanie's and his own. And you thought Vince was kidding when he said he wanted his children to follow him in the family business.

Hollywood has the casting couch. Wrestling, too, has its ways of separating the wheat from the shaft.

As long ago as the early eighties, dressing-room scuttlebutt ascribed a quickie National Wrestling Alliance title change to a blowjob that a certain promoter was allowed to administer to his short-lived young champion. In the last decade, Barry Orton, a second-generation wrestler now out of the business, claimed that his resistance to sexual harassment was the reason he never rose above prelim status. Another disillusioned ex-WWFer, Billy Jack Haynes, used to joke that he had to be careful about bending down for a bar of soap on the shower floor.

Vince McMahon's longtime right-hand man on the talent side was Pat Patterson, a former main eventer. Patterson's boyfriend, a "jobber" (perennial loser) called the Brooklyn Brawler (Steve Lombardi), had precious little else to recommend him. But that's just the start of allegations that Patterson has abused his power. Until recently WWF wrestlers talking about their moves in interviews would slyly allude to "the Pat Patterson go-behind." In wrestleworld this passes for sublime wit.

For former ring attendant Tom Cole it isn't funny. Understandably so. When Cole was fifteen or sixteen, he recalls, "Patterson would look at you when he was talking to you. He'd look right at your crotch and he'd lick his lips. He'd put his hand on your ass and squeeze your ass and stuff like that." Cole, now twenty-eight and a married small business owner, was speaking on the record. (Last year he also gave a detailed interview to the newsletter *Wrestling Perspective*, which can be accessed online at www.wrestlingperspective.com.)

Cole got started with the WWF around 1984 at the age of twelve, in Yonkers, New York, through Mel Phillips, then a ring announcer and head of the ring crew. Cole says Phillips had a black book with names of kids — mostly from broken homes — from all over the country.

"He used to have a thing where he played with your feet," Cole says. "He would wrestle you for five seconds, then he'd pull your shoes off and start playing with your toes. When I was a young kid, I wasn't thinking too much about it. Now I look at it like, 'Wow, that was a foot fetish. There's something wrong here.'"

In 1990, Cole says, Patterson's assistant Terry Garvin secured him a steady job at the WWF parts warehouse and promised him a tryout as a ring announcer. Garvin subsequently maneuvered Cole to his house, near the WWF's Stamford, Connecticut, headquarters, on an evening when Garvin's wife and two kids were away. Garvin popped a porn tape into the VCR and offered to fellate Cole, who declined and spent the night in a van parked outside. Shortly thereafter Cole was fired.

Cole first told his story to Phil Mushnick of the *New York Post* (and now *TV Guide*), the only mainstream journalist who has given the industry any kind of sustained scrutiny. In 1992, evidence of harassment and abuse of underage ring boys synergized with a federal grand jury investigation of McMahon's role in steroid trafficking among WWF talent. Hopelessly in over his head, Cole settled, on the eve of Phil Donahue and Geraldo Rivera shows devoted to the scandals, for $150,000, back pay, and the return of his old job. (Cole says his lawyer, Alan Fuchsberg, pocketed $100,000 of the settlement sum for "about four hours' work.")

At the height of the tabloid blitz, Patterson, Phillips, and

Garvin (who died in 1998) all left the company. But within a few weeks Patterson had quietly returned. Just over a year later the WWF fired Cole again because, he contends, he stopped sharing information from his grand jury testimony and refused to cooperate in McMahon's ultimately unsuccessful libel suit against Mushnick and the *Post*.

Not all of wrestling's legal-sexual problems stem from homosexual conduct. In 1999 the WWF's former women's champion Sable (Rena Mero), a *Playboy* cover girl, filed a $120 million lawsuit claiming she was verbally assaulted and threatened by WWF personnel who had also tried to coerce her into baring her breasts on a pay-per-view show and participating in a lesbian "angle." The suit was later dropped. WCW has had several parallel pieces of litigation; the best known of them featured former valet Missy Hyatt and was settled in 1996.

Nor does every incident of male aggression stop at sex. In 1983 the girlfriend of then-WWF headliner Jimmy (Superfly) Snuka died from a blow to the head in a motel room near Allentown, Pennsylvania. Observers who have studied the case still question whether the death was accidental.

For the feds, naturally, the big enchilada was Vince McMahon. And when they smelled blood, accusers of varying degrees of probity came out of the woodwork faster than The Rock can ooze hip-hop attitude. One of them, Murray Hodgson, briefly employed by the WWF in a minor TV-announcing slot, claimed in a civil lawsuit that Pat Patterson had crudely propositioned him. But at the conclusion of Hodgson's videotaped deposition, his attorney, Ed Nusbaum, withdrew from the case.

"The WWF spent what I would estimate at around $100,000 in its private investigation of Hodgson," Nusbaum says. (Tom Cole believes that during certain periods he was tailed by WWF-hired detectives from the Fairfax Group, now DSFX.) "I was absolutely convinced by the evidence that emerged establishing that Hodgson was a lifelong con man."

A babyface Vince McMahon interviews Greg "The Hammer" Valentine as The Grand Wizard looks on

Around the same time, the WWF's first female referee, Rita Chatterton, came forward with a tale of having been raped by McMahon in the back seat of his limousine. Chauffeur Jim Stuart corroborated Chatterton's account and filed a lawsuit of his own, alleging that during his WWF employment he had been forced into witnessing the commission of crimes. Both Chatterton and

Stuart have since disappeared into the fog machine. Stuart's lawyer at the time, Frank Riccio, is not returning calls.

For McMahon's part, he relies heavily in such situations on Jerry McDevitt of the Pittsburgh law firm Kirkpatrick & Lockhart, otherwise distinguished by his representation of President Clinton's naughty ex-political consultant, Dick Morris. Ultimately the grand jury ignored the sex stuff and handed down indictments on charges that McMahon had brokered illegal steroid transactions for WWF wrestlers through a Pennsylvania doctor.

At a sensational 1994 trial in New York, prosecutors thought they were delivering the goods via the testimony of McMahon's former secretary, Emily Feinberg, the wife of a WWF script writer, a one-time *Playboy* model, and someone assumed to have spent time doing the nasty with Vince. Feinberg's performance under cross-examination withered, however. Some speculate this had something to do with the fact that, outside the courtroom, she had been pumped for information by one Martin Bergman, a notorious "fixer" who may or may not have been a TV producer, but who definitely was the husband of McMahon's lead defense attorney, Laura Brevetti. (Bergman also is the brother of Lowell Bergman, the *60 Minutes* producer who took on the tobacco industry and is portrayed by Al Pacino in *The Insider*.) In any event, a jury acquitted McMahon on all counts.

Now fast-forward four years. McMahon, heretofore a babyface TV announcer, calculates that he is of more value to his company playing the evil corporate boss in a feud with Stone Cold Steve Austin. And so, in one popular magazine interview after another, McMahon becomes the first imminent Wall Street tycoon ever to brag — falsely — that he was *convicted* on one count of conspiracy to distribute steroids. And the magazine writers buy it, giving Virtual Vince even more of an outlaw image than he deserves.

Book *that*, Kevin Sullivan.

"Stone Cold" Steve Austin

"Flyin" Brian Pillman

CHAPTER 5

THE SMART AND THE DUMB

In Which We Raise the Question, Is Anyone *Not* a Mark?

Adapted from my article for the February 1997 issue of *Spin*.

Perhaps the final membrane of Western civilization was pierced in November during the World Wrestling Federation's *Raw* on USA cable, when wrestler Brian Pillman used a 9 mm handgun to chase away his hated rival, Steve Austin, who was trying to break into Pillman's home.

As Dave Scherer, publisher of *The Wrestling Lariat*, later intoned, the Pillman-Austin incident violated the "unwritten code" that "you never, ever involve the use of a gun in a wrestling angle." Race-bait to your heart's content, parade role models who make Dennis Rodman look like Cardinal Bernardin — but *don't* flash gunpowder.

Of course, Pillman didn't really pack heat against Austin, any more than Jack Lord on *Hawaii Five-O* actually defused a bomb in the elevator shaft of the Ilikai Hotel while wearing one of those loud shirts. Pro wrestling's extracurricular TV "angles" are like the bouts themselves, playing fast and loose with *cinema verité* as well as with the Greco-Roman tradition.

Fueled by Reaganist deregulation and a Ramboesque cultural moment, wrestling became the pseudo-sport of the 1980s. WWF hypemeister Vince McMahon, the Michael Milken of junk entertainment, used a steroid-inflated action figure named Hulk Hogan to spearhead wrestling's most serious bid for the Disneyfied showbiz-marketing mainstream. Today McMahon is on bankruptcy's ropes, having barely escaped conviction in a 1994 federal drug-trafficking trial. Hogan is with Ted Turner's World Championship Wrestling, currently engaged in a no-holds-barred battle with the WWF for market dominance.

As infomercials for direct-mail products outstripped wrestling shows as sources of legal payola for local TV stations, WCW and the WWF were reduced to battling over Monday night cable ratings rather than sales of Rowdy Roddy Piper ice cream bars. The grunt-and-groan racket has largely crawled back into the slimy primordial demimonde from whence it came, and that suits the "smart" fans just fine. They always disliked the kidvid slickness of the eighties, preferring the "authentic" style of the sport's blood-thirsty, bargain-basement UHF days (epitomized today by one of the few remaining independent cult promotions, Philadelphia's Extreme Championship Wrestling, run by the artist formerly known as Paul E. Dangerously).

Unlike marks who must think that Randy "Macho Man" Savage delivers off-camera elbow drops to his ex-wife, the supposedly sophisticated fans of wrestling's current postmodern age profess to be able to distinguish truth from verisimilitude. Still, they're spellbound by the mystique of demystification; they get a rush from deconstructing the sleazy process by which wrestlers "work" the gullible public. (*Working*, or faking, is the opposite of *shooting*, or the real deal. The Pillman-Austin TV shoot of a shooting was a *work*, not a *shoot*.)

Feeding the appetites of fans smart and dumb are industry newsletters, telephone hotlines, and most recently, websites of wildly varying journalistic credibility. Together they add a quasi-documentary layer to the traditional pulp and glossy fanzines found on convenience-store racks.

"Kayfabe sheets," as some zines are known, parse the tactics of wrestling's bookers the way *The New York Times* follows the movements of Hutu gunmen. According to Dave Meltzer's *Wrestling Observer Newsletter*, WCW's *Nitro* on TNT "had a full point [ratings] lead at 3.0 to 2.0 when [WWF's *Raw*] did the tease where Pillman pulled out the gun and signal went out. Curiosity over that did make a significant difference, as the third quarter [hour] saw them neck-and-neck with a 2.8 rating. Most interestingly, despite the WWF's teasing to get viewers to stay tuned — and this shocked me — WCW for the final quarter . . . picked up to a 3.2, while WWF dropped to a 2.5. Bottom line: the angle worked, not nearly as well as the Bret Hart interview two weeks earlier, but it worked for a few minutes. But it was teased for too long in between segments and was a major turnoff with the WWF traditional kids' audience."

To paraphrase Ric Flair: "Wooooo!"

The *Observer*, which Meltzer started in 1982 when he was a San Jose State undergrad, is the original, and arguably still most authoritative, wrestling newsletter. The game's gray lady, it sticks to a rigid two-column, twelve-page desktop format, run-on sentences, and some of the most erudite analysis of international affairs (including those in Japan, where as many as thirty wrestling promotions flourish at any given time) since George F. Kennan served as U.S. ambassador to Moscow.

Wade Keller's *Pro Wrestling Torch* got into the act in 1987. Keller regards his sheet as a trade journal, like the *Observer*, but he incorporates the photos and graphics values that Meltzer disdains. "What I do from a reporting standpoint is as legitimate as what any journalist does," says Keller, who majored in economics at Macalester College in Minnesota. "The honesty level and depth of coverage blow away most sportswriting I see." Meltzer and Keller are believed to have about 4,000 subscribers each at more than $1 per head per week. Another measure of the sheets' impact was the series of death threats phoned in to newsletter writers by Jim Cornette (now a WWF personality) when his Smoky Mountain Wrestling promotion was going down the tubes a few years ago.

The Internet, with zero printing costs and even lower editorial standards, drove more than fifty wrestling newsletters into oblivion or cyberspace, leaving only the *Observer*, the *Torch*, the *Lariat*, and a couple of others. Almost all web wrestling content consists of rambling fan chatter mixed with recaps of televised matches. Some webzines blatantly pirate material from Meltzer and Keller. One typical Internet column, "Markin' Out With Kaye Fabe," pixelizes the likeness of its putative author, a cleavaged blonde who opines, "I'm really sorry that Brian Pillman didn't shoot that jerk Steve Austin. . . . I think the lovely Mrs. Pillman should sue [Austin] for terrorizing [Pillman] in his own home."

Whatever the state of wrestling's cable ratings, sex-and-drug scandals, and weapons arsenals, traditional journalistic outlets tend to stay aloof. A notable exception was *New York Post* (and now also *TV Guide*) columnist Phil Mushnick, whose early nineties exposés led to the federal investigation that nearly landed McMahon behind bars. For the record, I'm not related to Mushnick — though I was once subpoenaed by McMahon's lawyers (one of whom, Jerry McDevitt, now represents disgraced White House aide Dick Morris) in pre-trial jockeying over the promoter's libel suit against Mushnick and the *Post*. The suit was eventually dropped.

In 1995, a year after McMahon's acquittal in his criminal trial, Mushnick reported that the feds were looking into possible misconduct during the trial by McMahon's lawyer, Laura Brevetti, and her husband, Martin Bergman, who allegedly approached key prosecution witnesses while pretending to be a TV producer.

My favorite McMahon trial anecdote, however, was published in the *Wrestling Observer* and involved Afa Anoia, who used to wrestle as one of the Wild Samoans and now runs a training

*The Wild
Samoans: Afa
Anoia holds a
young fan*

school in Bethlehem, Pennsylvania, that feeds young talent to the WWF. Early in the proceedings, the 330-pound Anoia positioned himself in the gallery close to the jury box, directed his baby blues at the jurors, cupped his hands, and repeatedly mouthed the words, "not guilty." Showing the official authority all too lacking inside the squared circle, Judge Jacob Mishler told Anoia to knock it off.

That was a shoot, not a work.

Muscle & Fitness cover boy: Vincent Kennedy McMahon

CHAPTER 6

PIMPING IRON

McMahon Fought the Muscleheads, and the Muscleheads Won

This was the cover story of the July 1991 issue of *Spy* magazine (r.i.p.) – with, of course, Arnold Schwarzenegger on the cover.

If you have remote control, a cable hookup, and way too much free time, you know Vince McMahon. He's the tuxedoed, shellac-haired, Nautilized emcee of the syndicated program *Superstars of Wrestling*, the USA network's *Prime Time Wrestling*, and NBC's *Saturday Night's Main Event*, all produced under the aegis of the World Wrestling Federation (WWF).

McMahon's is an uncharismatic if he-manly TV presence; he's TV wrestling's Zeppo Marx, looking on deadpan while Hulk Hogan and Sergeant Slaughter shove fingers in each other's faces and pretend to argue. But like Bill Cosby and Merv Griffin, whose on-screen personalities are equally unpresumptuous, McMahon is actually a shrewd, tenacious businessman with a multimillion-dollar empire. TitanSports Inc., his $150-million-a-year company (and the parent company of the WWF), has a brand-new $9 million office complex in Stamford, Connecticut, complete with state-of-the-art TV-production facilities. In addition to the cable and network shows, there are nightly live wrestling exhibitions, and four-times-yearly arena extravaganzas broadcast over pay-per-view for up to $30 a pop. *WrestleMania V*, staged in 1989, grossed nearly $21 million. There are WWF videocasssettes, posters, toys, apparel, a *WWF Magazine*, even WWF ice cream bars, molded in the images of WWF wrestlers.

And there are WWF stars who have managed to cross over into more conventional realms: Rowdy Roddy Piper landed the lead in the 1988 movie *They Live*; last fall, Jesse "The Body" Ventura was elected mayor of Brooklyn Park, Minnesota; and Hulk Hogan has starred in both feature films (the forthcoming *Suburban Commando* and 1989's *No Holds Barred*) and a commercial for Right Guard deodorant. Add it all up and you've got an entertainment conglomerate of formidable financial might.

This apparently is not enough for McMahon. Having expanded wrestling's audience beyond twelve-year-olds and trailer-park rowdies to include parents and condo dwellers, and having outmaneuvered Ted Turner (whose World Championship Wrestling organization lags far behind the WWF in attendance, pay-per-view, and merchandising revenues), McMahon is now diversifying into *bodybuilding*.

The WWF kingpin's fetish for pumping up is evident whenever he and his aides gather at one of their houses to screen Turner's pay-per-view offerings. "During unimportant matches or interviews, Vince will go into another room with a pair of dumbbells," says a staffer. "He'll come back all sweaty, with his shirt off and his chest and arms all pumped up. One of the guys, currying favor, will invariably say, 'Vince, you look better than your wrestlers!', and he'll beam."

Last year, McMahon announced the formation of the World Bodybuilding Federation (WBF), which would do for Berry "The Flexing Dutchman" DeMey and Troy "Top Guns" Zuccolotto what the WWF had done for Andre the Giant and Randy "Macho

Man" Savage. At the inaugural press conference in January at the Plaza Hotel, McMahon introduced Tom Platz, a blond former Mr. Universe known in his prime as the Golden Eagle, and now the WBF's director of talent development.

"I look forward to the day," Platz said, "when a WBF superstar is on an airplane and a tall black man looks over and says, 'Hey, I saw you on TV last night. And that tall black man is Magic Johnson.'"

Waiting in the wings were thirteen male bodybuilders, the WBF's first signees, clad in black-and-neon-green jackets, skintight tank tops, and black boxer shorts. Tony Pearson, known as Michael With Muscles because of his resemblance to Michael Jackson, flexed for the gathered journalists and said, *This is the nineties.* We have the opportunity to show bodybuilding is a sport and an art form."

Danny "The Giant Killer" Padilla, a mere sixty-two inches tall, but with washboard abs, spoke about his seven brothers and sisters and his dog Bruno.

Mike Quinn, whose pectorals have the consistency of fibrocystic boulders, struck a few poses and shouted, "Get ready to rock 'n' roll!"

Platz promised WBF shows would be less stiff than other bodybuilding tournaments and would pioneer the use of theatrical values — implying that other shows were too naturalistic and understated. "We're going to take the characteristics inherent in these guys and *blow them up*," he said.

When asked if WBF contests would contain any elements of WWF-style pro wrestling, Platz, his voice firm, said, "No. The best bodies will still win. Our bodybuilders will *not* become professional wrestlers."

At that point McMahon glared at Platz, rendering the Golden Eagle a ninety-seven-pound weakling. Platz blanched and said, "Uh, what I mean is, uh, there won't be any body slams on the stage."

• • •

The bodybuilding world has its own history, older than the WWF's, and its own McMahonish control-freak impresario: Joe Weider. Weider (pronounced "weeder"), the son of a Jewish pants presser who emigrated from Poland to Montreal, has been in the muscle business since 1942, when at the age of nineteen he started mimeographing and circulating a newsletter called *Your Physique*. Along with his brother Ben, with whom he co-founded the International Federation of Body Builders (IFBB) in 1946, Weider is responsible for publishing the muscle mags *Muscle & Fitness*, *Flex*, *Shape*, and *Men's Fitness*, and for the superstardom of Lou (*The Incredible Hulk*) Ferrigno and, in his pre-Hollywood days, Arnold Schwarzenegger. (Were it not for Weider's mentoring abilities, young Arnold's quest for fame and Hyannisport credentials might have ended at the 1965 Junior Mr. Europe competition.)

McMahon's formation of the WBF was tantamount to a declaration of war on the Weiders, complete with a gangland-style opening salvo. The story unfolds, appropriately, in Chicago, where four months prior to the Plaza Hotel press conference, McMahon spent $5,000 to set up a booth at the Weiders' Mr. Olympia competition to promote *Bodybuilding Lifestyles*, the WBF's then-unpublished fitness magazine. The contest proceeded as expected: Lee Haney, Schwarzenegger's not-quite-so-bankable successor as the sultan of sinew, walked off with his record-tying seventh title, worth $70,000. As usual, some fans grumbled that Lee Labrada, the runner-up, had better legs, biceps, proportion, symmetry, and posing skill.

The weekend's most interesting moment actually took place offstage, where four of the twenty bodybuilders were disqualified for failing a drug test administered by International Olympic Committee-accredited technicians. The crackdown reinforced the Weiders' newfound scrupulousness on the steroid issue; a few months earlier, the IFBB had stripped Shawn Ray of the title he'd won in Columbus, Ohio, at the Arnold Classic (yes, such a thing exists) for a similar violation.

The closing ceremony, at Chicago's Arie Crown Theatre, was vintage Weider, full of lame, self-congratulatory Elks Club chatter filtered through a horrible audio system. The audience, a 4,600-strong collection of groupies, gym rats, and girlfriends of the aforementioned, paid little attention to what was going on onstage. Each of the competition's sponsors was allotted a few minutes to talk up its products. Tom Platz, the designated spokesman for *Bodybuilding Lifestyles*, said, "I have a very important announcement to make. We at TitanSports and *Bodybuilding Lifestyles* magazine are pleased to announce the formation of the World Bodybuilding Federation. *And we're going to kick the IFBB's ass!*" The audience fell silent, and leggy models in slinky black evening gowns and *Bodybuilding Lifestyles* sashes emerged from the wings to distribute handbills promising "bodybuilding as it was meant to be" — a code phrase, some thought, for "no drug testing."

Vince McMahon had thoroughly upstaged the Weiders at their own event, and he still had one more trick up his sleeve. That evening, when the bodybuilding contestants returned to their rooms at the McCormick Center Hotel, they found WBF contract offers slipped under their doors.

Ba-ba-ba-BING! Ba-ba-ba-BOOM! The war was on.

"I'm not angry — you can quote me," says Ben Weider, sounding not at all like a wronged crime boss who has just dispatched a lieutenant to deliver a fish wrapped in newspaper. "I'm not even disappointed. But let's put it this way: It wasn't a very sophisticated or very honorable thing to do."

To demonstrate his lack of anger, Ben has promised lifetime suspensions from the IFBB to any bodybuilders who sign WBF contracts.

"If we'd wanted to, we could have turned off Platz's microphone or stopped his people from distributing their literature," he says. "But what the heck, we let them have their fun."

A stumpy, mustachioed sexagenarian with a tanned, friendly

face, Ben tries hard to sound unworried: "Other federations have come and gone before. It took us a lifetime of dedication, sweat and blood, and millions of dollars of investment, to get where we are. We're a serious and — quote me — *ethical* sport."

Identified on IFBB stationery as "Ben Weider, C.M., Ph.D." — the C.M. for his membership in the Order of Canada, the Ph.D. for his honorary doctorate in sports science from the U.S. Sports Academy in Daphne, Alabama — Ben spends much of his time traveling around the world and cozying up to the dilettantes of sporting goodwill. (His oft-repeated slogan is, "Bodybuilding is important for nation-building.") He has earned his self-aggrandizing, for-profit organization shocking international legitimacy. The IFBB is now recognized by seventy-four national Olympic committees, has 132 member countries, and recently forged relationships with the Soviet Union and China.

Three years ago he was invited to address the executive board of the International Olympic Committee. "I was given only fifteen minutes to speak," he says. "You may be sure it was hard to condense forty-three years of hard work into fifteen minutes!" Alas, the board was not sufficiently moved to make bodybuilding a Summer Olympics event, or even an exhibition sport; but Ben is still working to make Olympic pumping-up a reality. A true Renaissance man, he is also a founding member of the Napoleonic Society of America and has co-authored a book, *The Murder of Napoleon,* which retails a Swedish dentist's theory that Bonaparte was poisoned with arsenic by a member of his entourage. Jack Nicholson controls the movie rights.

If Ben Weider is the IFBB's brains, Joe is its brawn. In 1951, when he was twenty-seven, he entered the Mr. Universe contest himself, just to prove that he practiced what he preached. Of course he was the only contestant in the tourney's history to compete with his legs covered by suit pants.

When he started printing his first newsletter in 1942, bodybuilding as we know it didn't exist; posing exhibitions were annexed to Amateur Athletic Union–sanctioned weightlifting contests, and the dominant muscle magazines were published by the York Barbell Company. But Joe was on a mission. In 1949 he moved from Canada to New Jersey to begin his entrepreneurial career in earnest, and now he rules a company that he claims grosses nearly $200 million a year, most of it in equipment and health-food supplement sales.

The magazines, glorified catalogs of Weider products, at first appealed primarily to consumers of gay porn. Some of the early titles, like *The Young Physique* and *Demi-Gods*, plumbed this theme quite explicitly. It took four decades and the 1977 documentary *Pumping Iron* for them to achieve mainstream, supermarket-checkout-line success. In 1980, *Muscle Builder*, the lead magazine, became *Muscle & Fitness*, and cover cheesecake was added to the beefcake. (The homoerotic undertones persist, however. According to a mid-1980s study by the Northeastern University sociologist Alan Klein, between 40 and 75 percent of the pilgrims to bodybuilding's mecca, Venice, California — home of Muscle Beach and the flagships of the Gold's and World Gym chains — still supported their lift-all-day lifestyle through gay prostitution and other forms of hustling.)

Inside the magazines it's an ongoing tribute to the Master Blaster, as Joe likes to be called: articles by, about, or pertaining to Joe; photographs of Joe with Schwarzenegger and George Bush, and of trophies and vitamin bottles bearing Joe's likeness — by one count, 224 references to Joe in a single 250-page issue of *Muscle & Fitness*. (The group's general-interest magazine, *M&F* has an international circulation of 600,000. *Flex* is aimed at hardcore bodybuilders. *Shape* is for women.) But far from a brutish authoritarian, Joe seems Captain Kangaroo–ish, almost avuncular, with a salt-and-pepper mustache and a wavy pompadour. "Strive for excellence," he writes, "exceed yourself, love your friend, speak the truth, practice fidelity, and honor your father and mother."

Hef has his mansion; Joe and Ben have a swanky office building in Woodland Hills, California, that features a twenty-foot-high waterfall on a marble wall. In the lobby is a bronze bust of the Master Blaster (Weider concedes it is actually a representation of his head atop the neck and shoulders of Robby Robinson, a veteran black bodybuilder).

Some former associates say Joe fixes his contests to suit the needs of his business empire. He practically admitted as much in 1970, when associates asked him why Schwarzenegger had won that year's Mr. Olympia title when Sergio Oliva, a black Cuban, had clearly had the better physique. Joe smiled and said, in his clipped Quebecois-by-way-of-the-shtetl accent, "I put Sergio on the cover, I sell x magazines. I put Arnold on the cover, I sell $3x$ magazines."

Bodybuilding receives only a smattering of TV coverage these days, mostly on cable. Network shows like NBC's *SportsWorld* no longer pick up the Mr. Olympia contests, largely because those tournaments are stiff and anachronistic. Rochelle Larkin, the founding editor of *Bodybuilding Lifestyles* (Vince McMahon dismissed her in March), says the Weiders "never grasped the significance of the fitness craze. Think about it. How many bodybuilders are well known to the general public? One — Schwarzenegger."

"We are what we are," Ben says. "If we wanted to make funny shows, we could make funny shows. We will not, for the sake of money, reduce bodybuilding to some kind of show business."

Show business is in Vince McMahon's blood. His grandfather was a boxing and wrestling promoter who started out in the 1920s. His father controlled much of the Northeast pro-wrestling circuit in the 1960s and '70s, when small-time promoters still divided the country into Mafia-like fiefdoms (a practice ended by the advent of cable TV and the deregulatory actions taken by the FCC). In 1982, two years before his father died, Vince bought out his stock in the WWF and began aggressively expanding operations across the country. Dick Ebersol, president of NBC Sports and original co-executive producer of *Saturday Night's Main Event* — which

"Rowdy" Roddy Piper

in its six years on NBC has consistently drawn a larger audience than the show it irregularly replaces, *Saturday Night Live* — calls McMahon "the greatest promoter since P.T. Barnum."

Despite McMahon's shaky beginnings in the field — he was behind the coast-to-coast screenings of the 1974 Evel Knievel Snake River Canyon Jump and the '76 mixed match between Muhammad Ali and Japanese wrestler Antonio Inoki — he has since developed into, depending on your estimation of his intellect, either a gifted ironist with a connoisseur's eye for camp, or a schlockmeister with genuine affection for B-list celebrities.

Or both. Late in 1984, he sent a camera crew to shoot, of all things, a *Ms.* magazine banquet. Cyndi Lauper, then in her music-video heyday and involved in a public shtick with wrestling personality Captain Lou Albano, received one of the magazine's Woman-of-the-Year awards. Another award went to Geraldine Ferraro, the Democrats' unsuccessful vice-presidential candidate that year. Lauper and McMahon's crew begged Ferraro and *Ms.* editor Gloria Steinem to film promotional shots for the WWF. Ferraro dutifully turned to the camera and said, as she'd been instructed, "Rowdy Roddy Piper, why don't you fight like a man?" Steinem recited an old WWF catcall about how Piper's kilts resembled a skirt.

Doubtless both women thought their spectacularly undignified promos would be seen only by a few insomniacs up at two a.m. A few months later, MTV aired a live broadcast of a Madison Square Garden WWF show in prime time; Ferraro's and Steinem's comments had been edited to give the impression they were in the crowd.

The scene at the most recent *WrestleMania*, which took place at the L.A. Sports Arena in March, was equally improbable. Marla Maples, Donald Trump's squeeze, conducted an interview with the Nasty Boys, a bad-guy tag team, and was guest timekeeper for

Jim Hellwig:
The Ultimate Warrior

the main event, a showdown between Hulk Hogan and Sergeant Slaughter. Willie Nelson, despite his ongoing difficulties with the Internal Revenue Service, was on hand to sing "America the Beautiful." George Steinbrenner debated with NBC football announcer Paul Maguire over the validity of the instant replay as a means of overturning referees' decisions.

But McMahon may have pushed his manic, low-culture sense of humor too far this time. *WrestleMania VII* had been moved at the last minute from L.A.'s Coliseum, which seats 100,000, to the Sports Arena, which seats 16,000 — advance ticket sales were slow, and the WWF had been criticized for exploiting the Gulf War. McMahon had rescripted the Sergeant Slaughter character as a Saddam Hussein sympathizer, and Hogan had been dispatched to visit U.S. military bases as a pro-America hell-raiser. McMahon tried to save face with a story about how fear of terrorism had motivated the move to the smaller, more easily guarded arena.

Even more than he relies on the allure of quasi-celebrity and mock violence, McMahon relies on endocrinology. The WWF encourages the young, money-hungry dumbbells in its employ to do anything they please to their bodies. According to Superstar Billy Graham, a retired WWF champ crippled by bone and joint degeneration from steroid use, and Bruno Sammartino, who has had a falling-out with McMahon, nearly all of today's WWF stars are "on the juice."

"I love this business, and it's really sad to see what's happened to it," Sammartino says. "With all the drugs they take, the guys now are like zombies."

Wrestler Jim Hellwig — a former chiropractor and onetime Venice Beach habitué who calls himself The Ultimate Warrior — is perhaps the ultimate example of the WWF's bigger-is-better ethic. Even though he can barely pose and mug without getting winded, last year Hellwig was given the lead in the WWF troupe when Hogan was temporarily detained by Hollywood commitments. "I eat the chemical toxins that other men fear," the Warrior huffed and puffed in one TV interview. Dave Meltzer, wrestling columnist for *The National* and publisher of a newsletter called the *Wrestling Observer*, now refers to Hellwig as The Anabolic Warrior.

The IFBB, on the other hand, has stiffened its position against steroids. The Weiders, in their quest to get bodybuilding into the Olympics (Atlanta, 1996?) are no longer afraid to suspend or punish their star athletes, as they did Shawn Ray. "We want bodybuilders to be seen as true athletes, not chemical athletes," Ben says. "Bodybuilding is not body destruction. Quote me."

The IFBB has also begun to fight back against McMahon. After the Mr. Olympia debacle in Chicago, Ben Weider issued an advisory memorandum to his employees. McMahon's bodybuilders, Ben pointed out, make as many as fifty promotional appearances a year — far fewer than pro wrestlers, but grueling for bodybuilders, most of whom appear in only a handful of shows annually. If a WBF bodybuilder wins the publicized prize money at an event, it counts toward his guaranteed salary and is not necessarily paid over and above it. Furthermore, WBF bodybuilders' percentages of earnings from licensed products, videos, and other merchandise are based on net profits rather than gross revenues.

But foremost among Ben Weider's criticisms of McMahon is that everything he touches turns to kitsch. "The opinion of most people is that wrestling as organized by the [WWF] has been turned into a circus," Weider writes in his memo.

To Ben and Joe's delight, the expected mass exodus of bodybuilders from the IFBB to the WBF has not happened. It also appears that the pro-wrestling boom that made McMahon a multimillionaire in the 1980s has crested. Pay-per-view revenues for the last two *WrestleManias* were significantly lower than the 1989 record, and live-wrestling gates have fallen from an estimated $43 million in 1988 to around $30 million last year.

Still, Vince McMahon presses on. Rumors are afoot that Lou

Ferrigno is about to end his seventeen-year association with the Weiders to sign with the WBF. McMahon is also wooing Cory Everson, a six-time Ms. Olympia married to an editor at the Weiders' *Muscle & Fitness*. The WBF's first live competition is scheduled to take place this month in Atlantic City at — naturally — the Trump Taj Mahal; another is promised for later this year, and at least four more are slated for 1992.

"I'm doing this for the athletes," McMahon has declared. "I just want to see them get a fair shake."

POSTSCRIPT

Time heals all rifts, including the one between Vince McMahon and the Weiders. The World Bodybuilding Federation quickly went out of business. Nearly a decade and a half later, at age sixty, a still-buff Vince posed bare-chested for the cover of the April 2006 issue of *Muscle & Fitness*. This formed perfect symmetry with the appearance on the cover of *Playboy* of WWE "diva" Candice Michelle, whose fifteen minutes of fame stemmed from her steamy thirty-second Super Bowl commercial for GoDaddy.com, which got edited by ABC censors.

"The Nature Boy" Ric Flair

IT'S A WWE WORLD, THE REST OF US ARE JUST LIVING IN IT

CHAPTER 7

HOGAN'S ZEROES

Hulkster Vitamins Come in Two Forms — Orals and Injectables

People, March 23, 1992

He is pro wrestling's first million-dollar man: a crossover star of pay-per-view, silver screen, and Madison Avenue whose glistening six-foot-six-inch, 290-pound physique, intense glare, thinning blond mane, and friendly growl have been used to endorse everything from an antiperspirant stick to kids' vitamins.

But now — *wham! thud! oof!* — several of Hulk Hogan's former ring cronies have delivered what, in wrestling terms, amounts to an off-the-turnbuckle clothesline: they claim Hulk, thirty-eight, bulked up for years on muscle-inflating steroids and abused other drugs.

Hogan has declined *People*'s repeated requests for an interview to address these charges, which threaten not only his good-guy image, but his King Kong–size earnings as well. (The three-time World Wrestling Federation champion grosses an estimated $5 million a year, much of it coming from such outside-the-arena

"Superstar" Billy Graham strikes a pose

enterprises as commercials, toys, and movies.)

Hogan's headlock on the public's affections actually began slipping last June, when Dr. George Zahorian iii, the attending physician for pro wrestling bouts in south central Pennsylvania, was convicted under a 1988 federal law that outlaws the distribution of steroids for non-therapeutic purposes. Among the steroid abusers Zahorian named during his testimony was Hogan. Federal Express records produced by government officials show Zahorian sent packages to several dozen wrestlers, including Hogan. Four of them testified that the packages they received contained steroids.

Despite the testimony, Hogan's lawyers managed to quash a subpoena for him to appear at Zahorian's trial, arguing that it would have invaded their client's privacy and threatened his livelihood. After the trial Hogan denied all, telling talk show host Arsenio Hall, "I am not a steroid abuser." He did admit to injecting steroids briefly in 1983 while under a physician's care for a torn bicep. Hogan gave the same account to *People* last October, but added, "It's like putting poison in your body."

Among Hogan's fellow grunt-and-groaners, his public denials of steroid abuse were a stretch even by wrestling's elastic standards. In January, two of his ex-colleagues, Superstar Billy

Graham (real name: Eldridge Wayne Coleman), forty-eight, and David Shults, forty-two, whose wrestling moniker was Dr. D, began making the TV tabloid and radio talk show rounds. While admitting to being ex-steroid users themselves, they claim Hogan also had more than a passing acquaintance with the synthetic hormone.

Graham, a former WWF champ, remembered when Hogan, using his real name, Terry Bollea, was playing bass in a rock band in 1976 and trying, without success, to climb into the ring. At 230 pounds he was big — but not big enough. He befriended Graham and began asking about steroids. "I saw him a year or two later, and he'd gained at least eighty to ninety pounds," said Graham, who claims Hogan spoke of tennis ball-size scar tissue on his hips, the result of repeated steroid injections.

"I injected him well over 100 times," says Shults, now a New Haven, Connecticut–based bounty hunter for bail bondsmen, who maintains he was introduced to steroids in the late seventies by Hogan, then billed as Terry "The Hulk" Boulder. In exchange Shults would offer the rookie tips on such things as how to project his ring persona believably in public, while helping him take the drug, which is injected directly into whatever muscles require enlargement.

"I regularly gave him shots in the triceps [back of the arms], where he couldn't reach himself, and also a few times in the butt," says the former Dr. D. "Sometimes he took 12 cc's three times a week."

"Hulk always bragged about steroids," says Joe Bednarski, who retired from his WWF career as Ivan Putski, the Polish Power, in 1986. "He'd say, 'Shit, I don't cycle [a practice in which users abstain for a while to let the body return to its normal state]. I don't get off of them. That's how I stay "over" [popular].'"

But his sympathizers think Hulk is being unfairly worked over for using a drug that, until recently, could be legally obtained by anyone.

"Who didn't do steroids?" says Ken Patera, a former wrestling

Moondog Spot and Randy Culley,
Moondog Rex

superstar and 1972 Olympic weightlifter. "The word came down from the pro-moters, especially [WWF owner Vince] McMahon, that you had to be bigger than life. The only way to do that was to take anabolic steroids."

McMahon, a bodybuilder who has acknowledged exper-imenting with the anabolic steroid Deca-Durabolin, re-torts, "I've never encouraged anyone at any time to take steroids."

But Hogan's drug abuse went beyond steroids, according to David Shults. He says Hogan also used cocaine, marijuana, up-pers, and downers. Shults's friend Randy Culley, who wrestled under the names The Assassin and Moondog Rex, confirms: "Me and Hogan ran around together. He was real bold about steroid use. And he also did Placidyl [a sleeping capsule], Quaaludes, co-caine." (So, reportedly, did a lot of others: at least five pro wrestlers have died of drug overdoses in the last decade.)

Billy Jack Haynes, a WWF performer from 1986 to 1988, recalls a harrowing car trip to Hogan's Connecticut home with Hulk and two other wrestlers after a bout at Madison Square Garden in 1987. "There was pot, alcohol, pill-popping. Hulk was going 70 miles per hour on the freeway, stoned out of his gourd," says Haynes. "I got mad at him for driving under the influence. We almost had a fight over it."

IS PRO WRESTLING DOWN FOR THE COUNT?

The New York Times, **Sunday Sports, July 7, 1991**

With the recent conviction on drug-trafficking charges of Dr. George T. Zahorian III, the physician who supplied anabolic steroids to Hulk Hogan and other professional wrestling stars, the final stage in the life cycle of one of the signature pop-culture phenomena of our times has begun.

Wrestling, which emerged overnight from the carnival fringe to the show business mainstream, may be about to crawl back into the hole from whence it came.

Zahorian was found guilty by a jury in Harrisburg, Pennsylvania, in the first test case of a 1988 federal law that made illegal the distribution of steroids for non-therapeutic purposes. Steroids, which helped turned wrestlers like Hogan from pseudo-athletes into freakishly muscular cartoon action figures, fueled the estimated $150 million kiddie merchandising empire of Vince McMahon, the owner of the World Wrestling Federation.

Now McMahon (who was, according to court testimony in Harrisburg by Zahorian, one of the people who used drugs pushed by the doctor) is striving to preserve the image of wholesome family entertainment he so ingeniously cultivated over the last seven years.

In its Barnumesque excess and its relationship to larger currents in business, government, and society, McMahon's rise has been prototypically American. The dull truth, cleverly concealed from his patrons in the East Coast media, was that wrestling actually peaked as a live-event spectacle in 1983 – this renaissance spearheaded by old-line promoters in Atlanta, Minneapolis, Charlotte, Dallas, and Tulsa, before McMahon was a major player.

But McMahon was the first to realize the potential of cable television to break the sport's traditional territorial fiefdoms and make possible a truly national marketing base. By 1985 the WWF was on NBC and CBS; by 1987 it was filling the 90,000-seat Silverdome in suburban Detroit and pulling in record pay-per-view numbers for a grudge match between Hogan and Andre the Giant. Competitors like Ted Turner, the cable mogul who owns World Championship Wrestling, a much weaker rival group, continued to stalk McMahon, but he remained the master of kitsch and mock violence, with an ear for the campy underside of the Reagan-Rambo 1980s.

Around 1989, however, the wrestling economy soured. Overexposure caused attendance to plummet, and the public was no longer as amused by McMahon's propensity for tasteless shtick. Earlier this year, *WrestleMania*, the WWF's biggest spectacular, had to be moved from the Los Angeles Memorial Coliseum to the much smaller Los Angeles Sports Arena, in part because of negative reaction to the way the Hogan-Sergeant Slaughter "feud" exploited the Persian Gulf war.

Pay-per-view buy rates – the percentage of homes that were purchasing the shows – were down as well, according to Dave Meltzer, publisher of the *Wrestling Observer*, although the universe of wired homes continued to grow. And cable operators were having better luck with other kinds of events, notably boxing matches.

As with the original wrestling resurgence in the late 1940s, the sport's larger historical role seemed to be to provide cheap, easy programming for a new medium, popularizing it for the delivery of more respectable forms of entertainment.

Like Elvis, McMahon was living off the residuals, as his parent company TitanSports generated more revenue from the licensing of dolls, video games, T-shirts, and ice cream bars than it did from the sale of tickets. He built a $9 million office complex in Stamford, Connecticut, to house a sparkling new television studio and post-production facility, but soon reached a dead end with what wrestling alone could deliver. Ever desperate for new product lines, he made unsuccessful forays into movie production and boxing promotion, and most recently started a professional bodybuilding circuit.

If indeed the Zahorian scandal finally puts the wrestling resurgence down for the count, the footprints the sport left were remarkable. More or less serious public affairs programming like *The McLaughlin Group*, a political talk show with John McLaughlin as host, owe their stentorian style of discourse to wrestling interview technique.

With regard to steroids, they can be found in legitimate sports, too, as Brian Bosworth, Ben Johnson, and Lyle Alzado have demonstrated. Bodybuilding, a junk sport in which steroid abuse is even more pervasive than in wrestling, produced Arnold Schwarzenegger – an even bigger celebrity than Hulk Hogan – whose appointment as chairman of the President's Council on Physical Fitness and Sports seems to be a classic case of the fox guarding the chicken coop.

Like Vince McMahon, they're all part of a world where appearance and hype are the undisputed tag-team champions. There's something comforting, and something disturbing, about the process by which wrestling manifests our worst instincts, then implodes and allows us to go guiltlessly about our lives. In the end, intelligent observers are threatened not by what's fake about it, but by what's real.

"Hogan isn't a bad guy," says Dave Meltzer, publisher of the *Wrestling Observer Newsletter*. "He works tirelessly for charities, [even] when the cameras aren't around." But by failing to fess up to past steroid use, Meltzer believes, "he revealed himself to be just another carny con man."

It's an image of Hogan sharply at odds with that of the loving family man (he and his wife Linda, thirty-two, have a daughter, Brooke, four, and son, Nicholas, two) whose name is licensed to sell a popular brand of kids' vitamins. As a result of the steroids scandal, the joke heard in hard-core bodybuilding gyms these days is: "Hulk Hogan Vitamins come in two forms — orals and injectables."

Yet Solaris Marketing Group president Barry Ross, whose company distributes the vitamins, rejects any slurs on Hulk's good name, adding, "We stand by him 100 percent." Although a spokesman for Hasbro (which offers a line of Hulk action toys) would not return *People*'s phone calls, the scent of scandal has not persuaded Gillette to cancel Hulk's Right Guard deodorant spots.

Hulk Hogan with Jimmy "The Mouth of the South" Hart

Still, the accusations of drug abuse may have already accomplished what WWF opponents Sergeant Slaughter and Andre the Giant could never do: toss the Hulkster out of the ring — permanently. As if sensing his superstar's career is kaput, McMahon is pumping up Hogan's *WrestleMania VIII* bout against Sid Justice in the Indianapolis Hoosier Dome on April 5 as Hulk's last match before a "hiatus" that McMahon says "could be six months or six years, or forever, I don't know."

It is doubtful, though, that any such hiatus will be the end of Hulk's career. He has a standing offer to wrestle in Japan, where he can take home a six-figure payout for just a few bouts (and where steroid use by wrestlers is relatively uncommon). Still, the price of any such banishment will be felt not so much by the Big Guy as by the little guys — the legions of Hulkamaniacs not yet ten years old.

Sayonara, Hulk? Say it ain't so.

Randy "Macho Man" Savage and Jake "The Snake" Roberts

CHAPTER 8

SCANDAL SNAPSHOTS

A Dressing Room Raid by Federal Narcs — Plus Other Stuff They Don't Tell You About on *SmackDown* and *Raw*

These are excerpts of my regular reports for the *Village Voice* sports section's "Jockbeat" in the late 1980s and early '90s.

AUGUST 30, 1988

If Vice President George Bush knows "how to kick a little ass out there" (as he was said to characterize his performance in the 1984 debate with his Democratic opponent Geraldine Ferraro), you might think it's because he learned from mondo ass-kickers (and Bush buddies) like pro wrestlers Wahoo McDaniel and Ernie "The Cat" Ladd — or from campaign manager and Jake "The Snake" Roberts fan Lee Atwater. In fact, it's the other way around.

Back in the early 1950s, the veep coached the fledgling Wahoo in Pony League baseball in Midland, Texas. Wahoo, who is part Choctaw Indian and wears a war bonnet every time he enters the ring, later went on to become one of the headline attractions for

National Wrestling Alliance promoter Paul Boesch in Houston. When Bush ran for Congress in 1966, he asked his old chum and contributor Boesch to arrange for Bush to be in the ring for the main event of his next show, which happened to be Wahoo. After standing shoulder to shoulder with him, Bush put on Wahoo's war bonnet.

Bush won the election by a comfortable margin.

FEBRUARY 21, 1989

According to the front page of last Friday's *New York Times*, one of the most popular holds in pro wrestling today is the "chicken wing" — a move that went out with former champ Bob Backlund. The banty-necked pencil pushers at *The Times* also missed the real scoop behind the New Jersey wrestling deregulation debate: it also may be a tax dodge.

You don't have to be Bobby "The Brain" Heenan in order to figure out the reason World Wrestling Federation hypemeister Vince McMahon is lobbying desperately to get out from under the jurisdiction of that state's Athletic Control Board before April 2, when *WrestleMania* will be staged in Atlantic City. New Jersey's 3 percent athletic tax applies not only to the live gate (which Donald "Cock-of-the-Boardwalk" Trump has guaranteed the WWF will reach at least $2 million), but also to nationwide pay-per-view and closed-circuit revenues (projected to total another $18 million). So the Barnum of Bounce apparently hopes to chicken out of a possible $600,000 Jersey tax bill by frying the board's gizzard.

By the way, many people on this planet wonder whether The Lovely Elizabeth will fly the coop with Macho Man Savage or Hulk Hogan. Well, Liz Poffo is legally Savage's chick; Hogan is also married, and has a Hulkette.

AUGUST 22, 1989

The World Wrestling Federation's Vince McMahon has been the Big Bossman of "sports entertainment" for almost as long as Hulk Hogan has been bald, so it came as a shock when the Barnum of Bounce deigned to appear on *Entertainment Tonight* to talk about his promotional war with Ted Turner's National Wrestling Alliance.

Our Deep Chokehold reports that Vince had little choice: *ET* had threatened to use freeze-frame video from NBC's *Saturday Night's Main Event* that showed the *real* Big Bossman (former Georgia prison guard Ray Traylor) scraping a razor blade across his forehead to draw blood during a steel-cage match with Hogan last June.

"Juicing" is common in wrestling, but stars of the image-conscious WWF are never supposed to do it on network. The speculation is that McMahon took a stab at a little "color" this time because he's now running *Main Event* on his own. Former co-producer Dick Ebersol, the man who brought wrestling back to network TV after thirty years, used the show's success to get himself bumped upstairs to the presidency of NBC Sports.

Outraged by the juice over his airwaves, NBC entertainment chief Brandon Tartikoff verbally hip-tossed McMahon for being such a gross-out, and ordered him to cooperate with *ET*, which agreed to can the tape once Vince did the interview.

ET executive producer David Nuell confirmed the existence of the footage but insisted it was inconclusive. "Initially our researchers thought they had seen a blade, but I didn't see it," Nuell told us. Both Nuell and Tartikoff denied any intercession by NBC brass. "I'd like to take credit for getting Vince on my own," said Nuell. "We go back together ten years — I was at the NBC station in Washington when it carried his father's wrestling show."

Hell, we always knew *ET* wasn't fake journalism — it's every bit as genuine as prime-time wrestling.

OCTOBER 16, 1990

From Mexico — where pro wrestling is called *Lucha Libre* and the good guys and bad guys are known, respectively, as *técnicos* and *rudos* — comes the most disillusioning news since the Adorable Bruce Ritter was defrocked by the World Saints Federation. Fray Tormenta, a popular masked *técnico* with a real-life gimmick (he's a priest whose wrestling earnings subsidize an orphanage), has been arrested and charged with physical and sexual abuse of boys in his custody, and with selling some of them to homes in the U.S., France, Germany, Spain, and the Netherlands. Gee, what will we find out next — that the Ultimate Warrior does steroids?

JANUARY 3, 1991

Village Voice Sportswriters' Poll — Top Sporting Moments of 1990

We couch potatoes were familiar with the formula. After a few minutes of pathetic pantomime, Hulk Hogan summons the stamina and agility of a winded centipede to spring off the ropes with all 305 — well, 270 — pounds and drop a thigh on his victim's chest. Then *one, two, three* . . . Hulkamania lives!

But on April Fool's Day, at *WrestleMania VI* in the Toronto SkyDome, the joke was on us. The Hulkster was planning to spend more time with his family and make movies, and a former chiropractor who bills himself as The Ultimate Warrior was being groomed to become the new steroid superstiff. So this time the Warrior rolled away from the legdrop, nailed his own splash off the ropes, and pinned the champ in the middle of the ring — the first "clean job" Hogan had agreed to do since his Japanese tour in 1983, a year before Connecticut impresario Vince McMahon turned him into history's highest-hairlined kiddie cartoon hero.

Between Hogan and the Warrior, of course, there isn't enough athletic talent to fill Ric Flair's jockstrap, let alone Lawrence Taylor's nostril. Even so, clever "booking" and well-timed choreography made this the most stunning *circus* of a year without much *panis*. It also brought down the curtain on eighties excess as surely as Milken's prison sentence or Trump's divorce. The Warrior was a spectacular flop as wrestling suffered possibly its worst box-office cycle ever — even if pay-per-view and merchandising deals have so far kept McMahon from spilling fiscal blood. Crowds are way down even at the Garden, where sellouts had been a gimme since Bruno Sammartino was champ and Gorilla Monsoon was the first Manchurian expatriate to teach high school biology in Jersey. Say your prayers and eat your vitamins.

FEBRUARY 5, 1991

If wrestling fans are wondering what flabby-at-age-forty-two Bob Remus, alias Sergeant Slaughter, is doing back in the ring with a world championship belt after his 1984 contract dispute with World Wrestling Federation primo Vince McMahon — well, those weekly $6,000 WWF paychecks go a long way toward putting Remus's two daughters through college.

But the price of his return? Remus has to do a new shtick wherein superpatriot Slaughter, now unhinged by the end of the Cold War, has aligned traitorously with Iraq's General Adnon.

A perverse footnote to all this: The general's real name is Adnan el-Kaissey, and he's a legit native of Iraq who, in '58–'59, was an all-American wrestler at Oklahoma State.

FEBRUARY 12, 1991

Vince McMahon's World Wrestling Federation will announce Thursday that *WrestleMania VII* on March 24 has been moved from the 100,000-seat Los Angeles Coliseum to the 15,500-seat L.A. Sports Arena. Blowing characteristic smoke, the WWF will ascribe the switch to security concerns, but here's the real reason: The "angle" in which the villainous Sergeant Slaughter plays an Iraqi sympathizer has gone over with the public about as well as a Scud missile in Haifa.

Two weeks ago, after *National* wrestling columnist Dave Meltzer clotheslined him for poor taste, McMahon orchestrated a heavy-handed fax-and-phone campaign to get *National* editor Frank Deford to can Meltzer. Deford, however, not only backed his reporter, but also ran a follow-up story with rare on-the-record critical comments by wrestling industry insiders.

Now comes word that, seven weeks out, only 12,000 tickets have been sold for WrestleMania, in which Hulk Hogan is slated to squash Slaughter for God and country. So it's a seven-figure financial Baath for the maestro of "sports entertainment," who has already seen live-show revenues plunge from an estimated $43 million in 1989 to just $15 million last year.

JULY 9, 1991

World Wrestling Federation musclehead-in-chief Vince McMahon is doing heavy lifting on the propaganda front to keep the scandal surrounding Dr. George Zahorian — the WWF steroid connection who last week was convicted on twelve drug-trafficking counts in Pennsylvania federal court — from tarring the WWF's $150-million-a-year kiddie merchandising operation.

Zahorian acknowledged supplying the stuff to many WWFers, including Hulk Hogan, Rowdy Roddy Piper, and Bossman McMahon himself. Now Zahorian and McMahon are bracing for a possible civil suit by retired champ Superstar Billy Graham, who is crippled by bone and joint degeneration, he says, from the steroids pushed on him.

Meanwhile Hogan canceled most of his bookings last week with the lame excuse that he had a neck injury, and McMahon tried to distance himself from the former Pennsylvania State

*Ex-WWF champ
Bob Backlund*

Athletic Commission–appointed attending physician. "Neither the WWF, nor any of its wrestlers *or associates*, has been charged with any illegality [italics added]," Federation henchman Basil DeVito said in a statement full of enough sleazy half-truths to part Don King's hair.

DeVito failed to mention that in the early eighties, when WWF TV shows were taped in Allentown, Zahorian was part of the repertory company, frequently playing in the hyped-up skits known in carny lingo as "angles." (In his most tasteless angle, in 1983, Zahorian counseled Eddie Gilbert, who had just come back from a broken neck sustained in a car accident, that he might never wrestle again after The Masked Superstar "injured" Gilbert with a reverse neckbreaker — a scenario that moved then–WWF champ Bob Backlund to tears, and set up a series of Backlund-Superstar grudge matches.)

Back in the so-called real world of journalism, we wonder how *Sports Illustrated* plans to wipe the carbohydrates off its face a mere three months after running a puffy profile of McMahon by William Oscar Johnson that all but declared him the second coming of Walt Disney. On the eve of the trial, *SI* asked *Wrestling Observer* publisher and former *National* columnist Dave Meltzer to send a lengthy file on steroids and wrestling. Among other things, it repeats the oft-told joke among insiders that, under the wwf's drug-testing policies, you get suspended if you test either positive for cocaine or negative for steroids, and recounts instances of finding discarded hypodermic needles backstage at wwf shows. But Meltzer's report was reduced to a brief Scorecard item in the issue that hits the stands this week.

JULY 23, 1991

The world may be secure in the knowledge that World Wrestling Federation attending physician Dr. George Zahorian stands convicted of selling drugs to wrestlers, but is it ready for wwf steroid testing — what the wwf calls an "innovative" new policy to supplement what has been, since 1987, "the most comprehensive and enforced drug program in all of professional sports"?

Ready or not, details were to be announced by wwf impresario and positively id'd steroid freak Vince McMahon at a Tuesday press conference at pal Donald Trump's Plaza Hotel. Sources offer the following scorecard on four years of wwf cocaine testing (itself a PR stunt concocted after an embarrassing incident in which Hacksaw Jim Duggan and The Iron Sheik were busted for marijuana and cocaine possession in New Jersey):

- Tully Blanchard, co-holder of the wwf tag-team championship who flunked his test — suspended for several weeks.

- Jake "The Snake" Roberts, main-eventer who twice flunked — suspended each time for six weeks, resulting in a string of no-show bookings for which his fans never got an explanation.

Meanwhile, back at the box office, Hulk Hogan's bankability continues to get as flabby as his muscle tone will be once the 'roids wear off. A heavily hyped show at Busch Stadium last weekend drew a miserable crowd of only 14,500. In many markets, the August issue of the kids' magazine *Disney Adventures*, featuring an interview plugging Hogan's new movie *Suburban Commando*, is landing on newsstands with a new cover sans the Synthetic American. And Hogan has been pulled from most of his promotional appearances for the flick, now slated for a fall release. Don't be surprised if the next gambit from damage-control central is a tearjerker appearance on *Arsenio* in which His Hulksterhood confesses past sins and urges youngsters to keep following his example of "training, saying your prayers, eating your vitamins."

JULY 30, 1991

Going to the mat with that hard-hitting interviewer Arsenio Hall, a visibly nervous Hulk Hogan last week used what is known as the "Bosworth Defense" to deflect revelations that he was a heavy steroid user. The Bosworth Defense is named after football linebacker Brian Bosworth, who is suspected of using anabolic steroids to become a star in college before flopping in the pros. Bosworth said he used steroids only under a doctor's supervision, to treat injuries.

Similarly, Hogan on *Arsenio* owned up only to the brief use of therapeutic steroids for three injuries sustained circa 1983, even though convicted drug pusher and former World Wrestling Federation attending physician George Zahorian testified this month that Hogan was on the juice as recently as two years ago.

The Synthetic American also told Arsenio that the National Football League's steroid-testing program "has a hole in the bucket a mile long" and added, "I wish the NFL would adopt [WWF boss] Vince McMahon's new drug policy."

This bizarre juxtaposition came on the heels of McMahon's smoke-and-mirrors press conference at the Plaza — from which perceived unfriendly media, including the *Voice*, were barred — where McMahon admitted past "experimentation" with the anabolic steroid Deca-Durabolin. Whatever one can say about the NFL's drug policy, the WWF still doesn't *have* a policy; at this point it merely has had conversations with consultants from the NFL, the National Basketball Association, Major League Baseball, and the National Collegiate Athletic Association.

But let's cut the crap. As wrestling newsletter publisher Dave Meltzer says, "When we see all of these guys lose thirty pounds, then we'll know they are serious."

SEPTEMBER 24, 1991

The time limit is about to expire on World Wrestling Federation spin-control maven Vince McMahon's negotiations to forestall an expected lawsuit by a forty-eight-year-old former WWF champion who claims long-term abuse of steroids left him a functional cripple.

Last month, Superstar Billy Graham (real name: Wayne Coleman) offered to settle for $1.25 million, but McMahon refused and threatened to countersue if Graham filed, as originally planned, on the eve of *SummerSlam*, the WWF's recent pay-per-view show from Madison Square Garden. Onetime WWF attending physician Dr. George Zahorian — convicted in June on federal drug-trafficking charges for supplying 'roids to, among others, McMahon and Hulk Hogan — would also be named in the suit.

OCTOBER 1, 1991

The Von Erich wrestling family — a weird clan of born-again Christians who were hot box office in Dallas in the early eighties — suffered yet another apparent suicide last week: twenty-one-year-old Chris, the youngest son of overbearing patriarch (and Reverend Pat Robertson pal) Fritz Von Erich.

A five-five runt with no athletic ability and even less business being a wrestler than his older brother Mike (who killed himself with sleeping pills in 1987), Chris shot himself in the head just outside his parents' home near Tyler, Texas. Another brother, David, OD'd on sleeping medication during a Japanese tour in 1984.

Of the two surviving siblings, Kerry now works in the World Wrestling Federation as The Texas Tornado. But Kerry (who wrestles with a partially amputated foot, the result of a 1986 motorcycle accident) has been sidelined for the last two weeks because he's reportedly passing blood in his urine, perhaps from a bruised kidney suffered in a recent match. Kidney malfunction, of course, is also a symptom of steroid abuse.

OCTOBER 22, 1991

Hulk Hogan, who continues to claim he never used anabolic steroids and that convicted drug dealer Dr. George Zahorian only briefly prescribed corto-steroids for him as therapy for an early-eighties injury, received at least nine Federal Express packages from Zahorian between February and November 1988 alone, according to a computer summary of the doctor's FedEx records prepared by the U.S. Department of Health and Human Services' office of steroid investigations.

The packages, ranging from one to three pounds, were addressed variously to H. Hogan, Terry Bollea (Hulk's real name), Linda Bollea (his wife), and "Tiny Bolen" (a misspelling of the stage name of one of his former heel opponents) at his homes in Stamford, Connecticut, and St. Petersburg, Florida. The receipts were signed by either Linda or the Hulkster himself, who's now back on the talk-show circuit promoting his new flick, *Suburban Commando.*

Here's a free question for *CBS This Morning* cream puff Harry Smith the next time the Synthetic American is invited on the show. What was in those packages from Zahorian, Hulk? Three-pound vitamin bottles? Annual reports from Toys R Us and Gillette? Fan letters from little kids?

NOVEMBER 26, 1991

Five months after federal court testimony fingered him as a steroid abuser, Hulk Hogan's pee-pee was finally tested for 'roids for the first time last Wednesday, prior to a World Wrestling Federation show in New Haven. And what a surprise: The Hulkster now suddenly looks like a 297-pound weakling — sagging skin, shrunken chest and arms, gut drooping like a pro bowler gone to seed. Barring a last-minute change of plans, look for the Synthetic American to drop his wwf championship to The Undertaker at the *Survivor Series* pay-per-view on Thanksgiving.

MARCH 3, 1992

The World Wrestling Federation achieved another first in family-oriented sports entertainment when a local police dog and plainclothes narcs screened the bags of all wrestlers as they filed through the stage entrance for a February 14 show at the St. Louis Arena. The search came up empty after word of the raid reportedly leaked to the wwf through building management. The vice cops denied any connection to a possible federal Drug Enforcement Administration investigation, which has been much speculated upon following last summer's conviction of wwf steroid wholesaler Dr. George Zahorian; they said they were simply acting on an isolated tip about a particular wrestler and cocaine.

Meanwhile Kerry Von Erich, mysteriously absent from the WWF tour, got himself arrested in Richardson, Texas, on two felony counts of attempting to use forged prescriptions.

And compounding the latest drug scandal were charges by former prelim boy Barry Orton (a.k.a. Barry O) on a nationally syndicated radio show out of KVEG Las Vegas that he had been sexually harassed, casting-couch-style, by one of hypemeister Vince McMahon's top honchos.

All this may help to explain McMahon's testiness when, on February 13, he telephoned ex-*National* editor Frank Deford to complain about an ESPN radio commentary three days earlier, in which Deford urged Hulk Hogan to come clean about steroid and cocaine abuse. According to Deford, McMahon screamed, "I have proof I'm not a mobster!" — even though Deford had never even broached the subject. Shades of Richard Nixon, who in the thick of the Watergate scandal once addressed Governor Evans of Washington as "Governor Evidence."

MARCH 10, 1992

The scandal-racked World Wrestling Federation, coming off a February to forget, finds no relief in March. First up: a lengthy investigative piece by *Los Angeles Times* associate sports editor John Cherwa — expected to run some time this week — on Hulk Hogan's alleged use of steroids and other pharmaceutical tag-team partners. That will be followed by a series by Jeff Savage of the *San Diego Union Tribune*, dealing not only with drugs but also with charges (first reported last week by the *Post*'s Phil Mushnick) of sexual exploitation involving top WWF officials, underage ring attendants, and other employees.

On March 13, ABC's *20/20* has scheduled a segment on the

larger national steroid problem that will include the airing of Superstar Billy Graham's widely corroborated accounts of the Hulkster's abuses. (Hogan denies the charges made in the *Times* and *20/20* stories, maintaining he used only doctor-prescribed steroids to treat sports-related injuries.)

On the financial side, Vince McMahon, bossman of perhaps the only major entertainment company in the world with an unlisted phone number (to which Jockbeat's calls again went unreturned), faces impending disaster. Ticket sales for *WrestleMania VIII*, slated for the 75,000-seat Indianapolis Hoosier Dome on April 5, have stalled at around 15,000.

The real question seems to be how quickly corporate sponsors like Gillette and Hasbro will head for the tall timber. "The WWF is finished as an important name in kids' products," says Woody Brown, of Gary Caplan, Inc., a Cherry Hill, New Jersey, licensing firm. "It went into 1992 at a low level, and now it's simply managing its decline. But if a public scandal takes hold, you'll see their stuff drop off a cliff instead of riding down a nice, easy curve."

Also pumping down is the year-old sister World Bodybuilding Federation, which got no takers for a proposed new syndicated TV program — leaving muscle freak McMahon without a significant revenue stream from which to pay out millions of dollars in guaranteed contracts to, among others, Lou Ferrigno.

MARCH 17, 1992

Letter to the editor by Steve Planamenta, Director of Media Relations, World Wrestling Federation, Stamford, Connecticut.

"An item in the March 10 Jockbeat column contained several inaccuracies. First, it stated that our phone number is unlisted. If you call telephone information in Connecticut you will find our corporate number is listed, and was long before your item ran.

Second, you stated *WrestleMania VIII* tickets 'have stalled at around 15,000.' To the contrary, ticket sales proceed apace and are on target for our projections! Third, Gillette and Hasbro are not sponsors. Fourth, you quoted an employee of Gary Caplan Inc. implying that our licensing program is declining. To the contrary, we had an excellent fourth quarter and a strong start to the first quarter. Fifth, you state there were 'no takers' for our World Bodybuilding Federation TV program. Not true. Several stations committed to clearing the program but we opted to air it on USA Network (it debuts April 4 at 11 a.m.). Finally, you stated we have to pay Lou Ferrigno a guaranteed contract. Lou Ferrigno is not under contract and we are not paying him anything."

Irvin Muchnick replies:

"Sources in the WWF told us only 15,000 tickets had been sold at the time of our report. Regarding the WBF TV program, the USA Network is cable, not syndication; if there were 'takers,' there weren't enough clearances to put the show into production. Lou Ferrigno did indeed leave the WBF just as the *Voice* went to press."

MARCH 17, 1992

While the World Wrestling Federation braces for the imminent filing of a lawsuit by an upstate New York family charging sexual abuse of an underage ring attendant by top WWF officials, Vince McMahon's lawyers are already defending against another suit for wrongful termination of employment, filed three weeks ago by twenty-nine-year-old Murray Hodgson. The action in Stamford, Connecticut, Superior Court also charges sexual harassment by McMahon lieutenant Pat Patterson, who resigned last week.

Hodgson says he was hired in July 1991 to be a special events announcer on WWF television shows, as well as the voice of the sister World Bodybuilding Federation. In court papers Hodgson maintains that on July 29, 1991, Patterson approached him and asked, "So you're the new guy? . . . So what do you taste like?"

Hodgson replied, "You've got the wrong guy."

Patterson: "Not if you want to keep your job, you don't. Think about it."

On August 20 Hodgson was dismissed, despite what he claims was praise for his work from his superiors. On August 29, he says, he met with McMahon, who explained that he just wasn't the right person for the job. Patterson was waiting for Hodgson when he emerged from McMahon's office. "Wouldn't listen to me, would you?" Patterson allegedly said.

Hodgson's attorneys are Ed Nusbaum and Richard McLean, who represented David "Dr. D" Shults when he was sued by ABC's John Stossel, after Shults slapped Stossell on *20/20* in 1985. (Stossel settled for $425,000, paid by the WWF.)

Scandal bibliography update: *People* will run a piece this week about steroid champ Hulk Hogan's pratfall from grace, and Geraldo Rivera's *Now It Can Be Told* is set with a story on the up-state sexual abuse suit.

MARCH 24, 1992

This week, we'll give Larry King, Phil Donahue, and Dan Rather a clear field for the World Wrestling Federation sexual harassment/pedophilia scandal and concentrate instead on drugs.

The latest hoot from WWF and World Bodybuilding Federation mogul Vince McMahon is his announcement that Dr. Mauro G. DiPasquale has been hired to conduct educational seminars on the dangers of steroids. "DiPasquale," says a bodybuilding insider, "is universally acknowledged as just about the world's foremost authority on how to beat drug tests." Indeed, in Gold's and World Gyms across the country, his 1987 book, *Drug Use & Detection in Amateur Sports*, is a bible second only to that samizdat classic, *The Underground Steroid Handbook*.

Though DiPasquale's book doesn't actually condone steroid use, here's one gem from it, under the heading "Current Trends in Escaping Detention": "While there may be some basis to the use of [various blocking agents] as aids to escaping detection, there are numerous compounds being used that may or may not have any effects on the detectability of anabolic steroids. For example, some athletes swear that using combinations of honey, vinegar, garlic, lactulose syrup, and antabuh (women tossing in depo-provera) allows them to take Anavar and aqueous testosterone up to three days before a drug-tested contest."

In the meantime, just how bad is the heat between McMahon and the Synthetic American himself, Hulk Hogan? This bad: Hogan is rumored to be telling friends he'll "do the job" for Sid Justice at *WrestleMania* (that is, allow Justice to pin him cleanly) and retire from the WWF. He has an offer to work eight dates a year in Japan for wrestling impresario Antonio Inoki's promotion for $100,000 an appearance.

APRIL 7, 1992

"Thanks, WWF, for seven years of love and kindness," said the full-page ad in last Sunday's *Daily News*, purchased by an organization called Community Mayors of New York, and heaping praise on the World Wrestling Federation for annual benefit performances said to have delighted a total of 126,000 handicapped children.

Through all the WWF's drug and sex scandals, the *News* remains Vince McMahon's unofficial mouthpiece via the ramblings of wrestling columnist "Slammer" (a.k.a. Hank Winnicki) whose columns serve as a weekly ad for 900-number entrepreneur Blackjack Brown's wrestling hotline.

Another WWF puff sheet, *USA Today*, which traditionally gets at least one full-page ad prior to *WrestleMania*, last week ran, in the same edition that quoted experts as saying steroid tests were beatable, a piece touting the WWF's "Look, Ma, no sanctions" steroid program.

At *Voice* press time, a report on Geraldo Rivera's *Now It Can Be Told* about the sexual abuses of WWF officials was scheduled to air April 3. McMahon would like to piledrive that broadcast into oblivion, and indeed the lawyer for former WWF ring attendant Tom Cole obtained a court injunction banning the show from using a previously taped interview with Cole. Two weeks ago, on the eve of a Phil Donahue symposium on alleged homosexual harassment and pedophilia in the WWF, Cole settled with McMahon for $50,000 in "back pay" and the restoration of his glamorous job.

APRIL 14, 1992

An even bigger waste of paper than *WrestleMania VIII* tickets was a widely circulated letter to WWF hypemeister Vince McMahon, dated March 23, from Dr. Anthony F. Daly Jr., the WWF's L.A.-based steroid-testing consultant. Daly says the initial steroid test (administered last November) showed a 50 percent usage among wrestlers, but all succeeding tests offered "no indication that any of the wrestlers have continued to use anabolic steroids."

Bullshit, says *Wrestling Observer* publisher Dave Meltzer: "Over the Christmas holidays many WWF wrestlers were banding together to discuss their right to continue using steroids. As recently as two weeks ago, another WWF steroid consultant, Dr. Mauro DiPasquale, admitted to me that there was still some use."

New York's ever-vigilant State Athletic Commission, of course, has taken no interest at all in the steroid problem — so we wonder if it'll act in any meaningful way on charges by former WWF ref Rita Marie (Rita Chatterton) that McMahon raped her, then fired her in 1986. (She made the statements on *Now It Can Be Told*; they were corroborated to Jockbeat by McMahon's ex-chauffeur, Jim Stuart, who says he was an eyewitness and has also filed suit against McMahon.) According to deputy commissioner Rich Hering, Chatterton began refereeing for the WWF in 1987 and continued to

1991 — an account refuted by millions of viewers of WWF matches taped in 1985–86 and of the USA network's defunct talk show *TNT*, on which she appeared with host McMahon.

JUNE 23, 1992

One reliable barometer of how serious World Wrestling Federation supremo Vince McMahon is about cleaning up the steroid problem in wrestling is whether he'll continue to push wrestlers to top positions on the basis of cartoon physiques.

Hawk and Animal: The Road Warriors

Well, front-office sources have leaked to us the following plans for the next pay-per-view show, *Summer Slam* (to be staged at London's Wembley Stadium on August 29 and shown here two days later):

- The Ultimate Warrior — also known to insiders as "The Anabolic Warrior" — will again become WWF champion.
- Legion of Doom — two Minnesota weightlifters who became overnight stars as the Road Warriors in 1983, and whose pumped look, along with Hulk Hogan's, is considered the catalyst of the contemporary steroid craze — will capture the tag-team championship.
- As for the projected losers — "Macho Man" Randy Savage, Bret "Hit Man" Hart, "Million Dollar Man" Ted DiBiase, and "IRS" Mike Rotunda — they're all respected technicians and "workers," but a little too small to "set the standard for drug-free sports and entertainment," as the current WWF slogan goes.

POSTSCRIPT

Sixteen years later, Fray Tormenta ("Friar Storm"), the *nom de garre* of the Rev. Sergio Gutierrez of Teotihuacan, just outside Mexico City, was the inspiration for the Jack Black character in the hit movie *Nacho Libre*.

Father Gutierrez was eventurally exonerated in the 1990 charges, which were said to have been instigated by a jealous former tag-team partner, the Bengal Tiger (Juan Ortiz).

Not all topical references stand the text of time: Bruce Ritter was a revered New York priest and advocate for homeless youth who fell from grace after the revelation that he sexually abused some of the boys under his wing.

A young Ted DiBiase

"Superfly" Jimmy Snuka

CHAPTER 9

SUPERFLY SNUKA &
THE GROUPIE

The "Wrestling Renaissance" Wasn't About to be Derailed by the Revelation That One of its Superstars Battered Women — One of Them to Her Death

In 1992 the *Village Voice* commissioned me to supplement my Jockbeat items about the WWF drug and sex scandals with a lengthy cover story. The article never ran, for complicated reasons, and I later won a court judgment against the *Voice* for payment of my full fee. Though the half-edited and obsolete main article doesn't stand the test of time for inclusion in this volume, I present here the infamous and equally unpublished "sidebar."

For Vince McMahon, the Hundred Million Dollar Man, Jimmy "Superfly" Snuka made for a challenging tag-team partner. The World Wrestling Federation's second-most-popular star in the early eighties, Snuka was an illiterate immigrant from Fiji prone to bouts with the law that threatened the revocation of his green card, and a drug abuser who often missed bookings. During a Middle East tour in the summer of 1985, fellow wrestlers say, customs officials in Kuwait caught him with controlled substances taped to his body, and he was allowed to leave the country only after some fancy footwork.

But Snuka's near–*Midnight Express* experience in the Persian Gulf was child's play compared to what happened on May 10, 1983. That night, after finishing his last match at the WWF TV taping at the Lehigh County Agricultural Hall in Allentown, Pennsylvania, he returned to Room 427 of the George Washington Motor Lodge in nearby Whitehall to find his girlfriend of nearly a year, Nancy Argentino, gasping for air. Two hours later, this twenty-three-year-old wrestling fan — who'd worked as a dentist's assistant in Brooklyn and dropped out of Brooklyn Community College to travel with Snuka — was pronounced dead at Allentown Sacred Heart Medical Center of "undetermined craniocerebral injuries."

"Upon viewing the body and speaking to the pathologist, I immediately suspected foul play, and so notified the district attorney," Lehigh County coroner Wayne Snyder told me on a recent trip to Allentown. In '83 Snyder was deputy to coroner Robert Weir. Yet no charges were filed in the case, no coroner's inquest was held, and no evidence was presented to a grand jury.

Officially the case is still open — meaning Argentino's death was never ruled either an accident or a homicide — though the original two-month-long investigation has been inactive for nine years. Under Pennsylvania's unusually broad exemptions from freedom of information laws, the Whitehall Township Police Department so far has refused my requests for access to the file.

Of particular interest would be two documents: the autopsy and the transcript of the interrogation of Snuka immediately thereafter. One local official involved in the investigation, as well as one of the Argentino family's lawyers, told me the autopsy showed marks on the victim other than the fractured skull. And former Whitehall police supervisor of detectives Al Fitzinger remembered that the forensic pathologist, Dr. Isadore Mihalakis, confronted Snuka to ask him why he'd waited so long before calling an ambulance. Gerald Procanyn, the current supervisor of detectives who worked on the case nine years ago, maintained that Snuka cooperated fully with investigators after being informed of his right to have a lawyer present, and was accompanied only by McMahon.

Another investigator, however, saw things differently; he said Snuka invoked his naïve jungle-boy wrestler's gimmick as a way of playing dumb. "I've seen that trick before," the investigator said. "He was letting McMahon act as his mouthpiece."

Another curious circumstance was the presence at the interrogation of William Platt, the county district attorney. According to experts, chief prosecutors rarely interview suspects, especially in early stages of investigations, for the obvious reason that they may become witnesses and hence have to recuse themselves from handling the subsequent trials.

Detective Procanyn gave me the following summary of Snuka's story. On the afternoon before she died, Snuka and his girlfriend were driving his purple Lincoln Continental from Connecticut to Allentown for the wwf taping. They'd been drinking, and they stopped by the side of the road — the spot was

Jimmy Snuka and "manager" Buddy Rogers interviewed for a WWF TV taping

never determined, but perhaps it was near the intersection of Routes 22 and 33 — to relieve their bladders. In the process, Argentino slipped on mossy ground near a guard rail and struck the back of her head. Thinking nothing of it, she proceeded to drive the car the rest of the way to the motel (Snuka didn't have a driver's license) and, after they checked in, picked up take-out food at the nearby City View Diner. Snuka had no idea she was in any kind of distress until he returned late that night from the matches at the Agricultural Hall.

Procanyn said Snuka's story never wavered, and no contradictory evidence was found.

Curiously, contemporary news coverage, such as the front-page account in the *Allentown Morning Call*, made no mention of a scenario of peeing by the roadside. It focused, instead, on the question of whether Argentino fell or was pushed in the motel room. Nine years later, the reporter, Tim Blangger, vividly recalled that at one point in his interview of Procanyn the detective grabbed him by the shoulders in a speculative reenactment of how Snuka might have shoved the woman more strongly than he intended.

Procacyn also claimed to have no knowledge of any subsequent action by the Argentino family, except for a few communications between a lawyer and D.A. Platt over settling the funeral bill. In fact, the Argentinos commissioned two separate private investigations, and it's difficult to believe that Procanyn was unaware of them. The first investigator, New York lawyer Richard Cushing, traveled to Allentown, conducted extensive interviews, and aggressively demanded access to medical records and other files.

"It was a very peculiar situation," Cushing told me. "I came away feeling Snuka should have been indicted. The police and the D.A. felt otherwise. The D.A. seemed like a nice enough person who wanted to do nothing. There was fear, I think, on two counts: fear of the amount of money the World Wrestling Federation had, and physical fear of the size of these people."

Even so, Cushing declined to represent the family in a wrongful-death civil suit against Snuka. The lawyer cited the fact that Snuka and Argentino weren't married, that they didn't have children, and that she wasn't working, which would make it difficult to establish loss of consortium. "Moreover, Vince McMahon made it clear to me that her reputation would be besmirched. As a lawyer, I had to determine if a contingency [fee] was in order; my business decision, not my moral judgment, was no. The family wasn't pleased. They had a typical working-class family's anger that justice wasn't done."

Through the generosity of Nancy Argentino's father's boss, the family then retained a Park Avenue law firm. The report filed by its private investigator shows that Snuka was as creative outside the ring as he was inside it:

- To the Whitehall police officer who responded to the first emergency call, Snuka said "he and Nancy were fooling around outside the motel room door when he inadvertently pushed Nancy and she fell, striking her head."
- An emergency room nurse heard him state that "they were very tired and they got into an argument resulting in an accidental pushing incident. Ms. Argentino fell back and hit her head."
- In the official police interrogation, Snuka first floated the peed-on-the-roadside theory.
- Finally, in a meeting with the hospital chaplain, he said he and Argentino had been stopped by the side of the road and had a lovers' quarrel: "He accidentally shoved Ms. Argentino, who then fell backwards hitting her head on the pavement. They then arrived at the motel and went to bed. The next morning, Ms. Argentino complained that she was ill and stayed in bed. . . . When he came home from the taping, he observed that Ms. Argentino was clearly in bad shape."

In 1985 the Argentinos obtained a $500,000 default judgment against Snuka in United States District Court in Philadelphia. The family never collected a dime; Snuka's lawyers withdrew from the case, stating that they hadn't been paid, and Snuka filed an affidavit claiming he was broke and unemployed and owed the IRS $75,000 in back taxes.

Since 1983, the forty-nine-year-old Snuka has been in and out of rehab centers and has wrestled off and on both in Japan and throughout this country. His original WWF stint extended two and a half years beyond Argentino's death; his most recent ended earlier this year. According to the wrestling grapevine, he's now trying to promote independent shows in, of all places, Salt Lake City, but my efforts to track him down there were unsuccessful.

Proving negligence, of course, is different from proving involuntary manslaughter or murder. But critics of the criminal investigation question the failure of the police to examine seriously Snuka's history of drug abuse and violence against women.

Former wrestling great Buddy Rogers, who'd been hired by McMahon to serve as Snuka's TV "manager" and get him to important matches on time, said he stopped driving with the Superfly after he brazenly snorted coke when they were in the car together. "Jimmy could be a sweet person, but on that stuff he was totally uncontrollable," said Rogers, who was also Snuka's neighbor on Coles Mill Road in Haddonfield, New Jersey. Snuka's wife, with whom he had four children, befriended Rogers' wife. "Jimmy used to beat the shit out of that woman," Rogers said. "She would show up at our house, bruised and battered. But she couldn't leave him — he had her hooked on the same junk he was using."

Nancy Argentino's younger sister remembered once being threatened by Snuka when they were alone at the family's home in Flatbush. "I could kick you and put my hands around your throat and nobody would know," he allegedly said. After Nancy's death, family members said, they received a series of phone calls from a woman who identified herself as a former Snuka girlfriend who'd tried to warn Nancy away from him. Snuka, said the woman, had once broken her ribs, and had a thing about pushing women back against walls.

Finally, there was the incident involving Snuka and Argentino at a Howard Johnson's in Salina, New York, outside Syracuse, just three months before Allentown. The motel owner, hearing noise from their room, called the police, who found Snuka and Argentino running naked down the hallway. It took eight deputy sheriffs and a police dog to subdue Snuka. Argentino sustained a bruise of her right thumb. Snuka pleaded guilty to violent felony assault with intent to cause injury, received a conditional discharge on counts of third-degree assault, harassment, and obstruction of a government official, and donated $1,500 to a deputy sheriffs' survivors' fund. Whitehall police later decided this was all the result of "a nervous desk clerk," Detective Procanyn told me.

According to attorney Cushing, McMahon made a remark at one point in their discussions that was at once insightful and chilling.

"Look, I'm in the garbage business," the promoter said. "If you think I'm going to be hurt by the revelation that one of my wrestlers is really a violent individual, you're mistaken."

Six months after Nancy Argentino died, the *Village Voice* ran a prescient article entitled "Mat Madness," by the late columnist Arthur Bell, weather vane of the lower-Manhattan gay-arts demimonde. After attending a Madison Square Garden show headlined by a bout between Superfly Snuka and The Magnificent Muraco, Bell — who knew next to nothing about wrestling — commented on the spectacle's graphic references to bodily functions, and on its barely sublimated undercurrents of sexual dominance and sadomasochism.

"Take my word," Bell declared with the confidence of a culture-monger paid to deliver big opinions, "by the end of 1984, wrestling will be the most popular sport in New York since mugging."

Bell concluded with a vignette at the Garden stage exit, where a swarm of fans, led by a woman named Bea from West Orange, converged to taunt the wrestlers as they emerged in their street clothes.

Snuka throttles ECW founder Tod Gordon

"Hey, Superfly," Bea shouted to Snuka. "You goddam fuckin' murderer. When are you gonna kill another girl?"

Superfly Snuka, in his sixties, is still kicking around. In his most recent WWE stint (more recent than the one referenced in the above
article from 1992) they even made a big deal out of his talking
openly about past problems with substance abuse (the same ploy
that would be used to help get Eddie Guerrero "over" just a year or
so before Guerrero was found dead in a hotel room). But, needless
to add, not even on this dose of "reality television" did Snuka or anyone else ever breathe a word about Nancy Argentino.

William H. Platt, district attorney of Lehigh County from 1976 to
1991, went on to become city solicitor of Allentown, and is now
president judge of the County Court of Common Pleas.

Sgt. Slaughter wants you!

CHAPTER 10

VINCE McMAHON, THE NEW BOB HOPE

Entertaining the Troops Abroad — Clamping a Sleeperhold on the Citizens at Home

From the December 27, 2004, edition of the San Francisco alternative newspaper *Beyond Chron*.

Just as Bob Hope used to entertain the troops in Vietnam, so today does Vince McMahon's World Wrestling Entertainment fill that role in the testosterone-bulked mutation of Vietnam we call the Iraq war. This week a special edition of the WWE's *SmackDown* show on the UPN television network, backed by a full-page ad in *The New York Times*, made the parallel unmistakable, as The Undertaker and Rey Mysterio plied their craft in rings set up on military bases, and McMahon solemnly promised our men in uniform that upon his return home, he would tell naysayers that "you said they can go straight to hell."

Though nowhere close to the popularity peaks it achieved first in the mid-1980s and then again in the late 1990s, pro wrestling has long been one of popular culture's most reliable Zeitgeist meters. And like his Connecticut-based predecessor

Phineas Taylor Barnum, Vincent Kennedy McMahon is about a lot more than just the axiom that a new sucker is born every minute. McMahon is our cheerful tour guide to the dark side of the American soul.

Those of us who have been fascinated by this pseudo-sport since we were knee-high to a turnbuckle have always known as much. Others — sociologists, serviceably trendy journalists, Parents Television Council-pandering senators, populist governors, action movie stars — either awake to it in cycles or exploit it in fashion. As with the Mafia's mirror on capitalism, the growth of wrestling from a carny demimonde to a national marketing base has rendered it exactly the same as the less marginalized aspects of sports and society, only more so.

Consider the layers of evidence of the thorough wrestlingization of our culture.

Debased political dialogue fueled by shouters on talk radio? Bill O'Reilly and Al Franken owe everything to heel-versus-babyface interview technique.

Crass transformation of group competition into individualized aggrandizement and vestigial spectacle? McMahon's alternative XFL football league was euthanized after one season on Saturday nights on NBC in 2001, but its currents run strong and deep. National Football League–licensed video games put more resources into extracurricular violence and "attitude" than into simulating the sport. Philadelphia Eagles wide receiver Terrell Owens' controversial *Monday Night Football* frolic with *Desperate Housewives* costar Nicollette Sheridan may as well have been a *SmackDown* promo.

Infiltration of performance and/or physique-enhancing drugs? Retired baseball most valuable player Ken Caminiti recently dropped dead, and others are sure to follow. But literally dozens of wrestlers in their twenties, thirties, and forties have dropped dead in the last two decades — a staggering epidimeological trail hidden in plain sight, noticed by few, cared about by fewer still. In the silver age of the American empire, death itself has turned into a punch line of the old commercial: "Is it live or is it Memorex?"

Finally, those of you who are outraged by the WWE's stunt in Iraq must understand that this is a bipartisan phenomenon, and more than a depraved metaphor. Lowell Weicker, onetime dynamo of the Senate Watergate Committee, sits on the board of directors of World Wrestling Entertainment, Inc. After its predecessor, a closely held family company, went public in 1999, Weicker profited handsomely from the sale of WWE stock. Earlier in the decade, Weicker, as governor of Connecticut, had helped burnish McMahon's image by appointing him to the board of the Special Olympics at a time when the Justice Department was investigating him on charges of drug trafficking and the harboring of a pedophilia ring. (McMahon later was acquitted in federal court of the drug charges; the grand jury never indicted him for anything else.)

Vince McMahon isn't through with us, nor are we with him. The marketing juggernaut he created will ride up and down a few more times, and it's impossible to predict whether he'll wind up as the toast of Wall Street or the next Martha Stewart behind bars. Our attention wanes at our own peril.

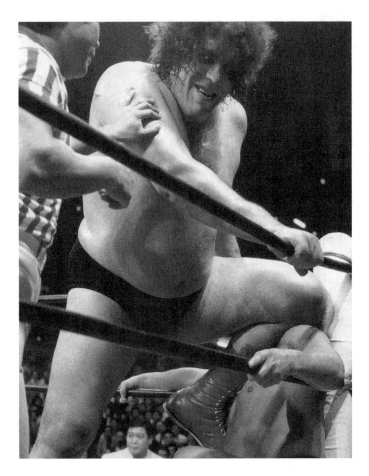

Wrestling legend Andre the Giant

DEATH MATCH, 1985 TO 2006

Greg Oliver, co-founder of the SLAM! Wrestling website and author of The Pro Wrestling Hall of Fame: The Heels *and other books, provided generous research support for this compilation. Thanks also to Brad Dykens of the "Obsessed with Wrestling" website.*

A 2002 article in the *International Journal of Sports Medicine* found that 62 powerlifters from Finland who were suspected of using anabolic steroids had died young at a rate five times higher than people like you and me.

In 2006 the Scripps Howard News Service, studying the records of 3,850 deceased National Football League players over the course of a century, determined that pro footballers "are dying young at a rate experts find alarming," with the heaviest athletes clocking in as more than twice as likely as their teammates to pass away before their 50th birthdays. The money stat: a total of 130 players born since 1955 – one in 69 – died, a fifth of them from heart diseases.

It is unsurprising that a lot less attention has been accorded the mortality rate of pro wrestlers; they're just, you know, *wrestlers*. (Truth be told, little more than crocodile tears are shed for assembly-line football players, too.) Even so, the empirical data are numbing and depressing – when the anecdotes are stacked up, the job looks as hazardous as a military billet in Falujah. During the two decades of the wrestling industry's spectacular growth in terms of both money and pop-cultural impact, its performers – a talent population skewed toward the big, the would-be big, and the all-around wacked-out – have been dropping like flies.

Don't hold your breath for a rigorous epidemiological survey. But below we take a baby step in that direction by documenting many (by no means all) of the wrestlers who have met untimely deaths in recent years. Defying my best efforts, the list below is staggeringly incomplete.

We use the same cutoff as the football study: fatalities under the age of 50. Beyond that, methodology gets tricky. Precisely what is a drug- or lifestyle-related death?

Maybe more importantly, at what point does a cluster of such deaths become an affair of state? Willie Nelson sang, "Mama, don't let your babies grow up to be cowboys," but that didn't stop him, in effect, from gambling – successfully in his case – that he would continue to create popular and acclaimed music long past the age of 29, which was how old Hank Williams was when he died drunk. Williams would have counted in our wrestling list because he was in the passenger seat of his car. But he wouldn't have counted if he had been in the driver's seat and crashed the car. To be sure, the latter phenomenon is a major occupational hazard for wrestlers, as it is for itinerant musicians, and is often a byproduct of impairment. But I'm not going to bother with that category of deaths here. It just isn't realistic to expect entertainment consumers to be motivated to vote with their wallets against any and all poor judgments glory-seekers might take in the name of their entertainment.

Nor, using similar logic, does this list get into training deaths, of which there also has been a good number. From there it's a slippery slope to investigating the alleged trend of "backyard wrestling." That's scary, to be sure, but of dubious pertinence. If I had a kid who felt compelled to dress up in a Superman cape on days other than October 31, I'd seal the second-story windows.

A case at least can be made that wrestling's drug pandemic is another matter. For one thing, it involves out-of-control use of borderline or illegal substances. For another, it's a problem that promoters themselves have the power to ameliorate by adjusting their awards system from the current one of "nothing succeeds like excess." Unless you believe that wrestlers somehow are not actual human beings, decency demands that we not interpret with laissez faire dismissiveness the role that institutionalized substance abuse plays in whatever more benign-sounding, generic causes medical examiners might be trained or cajoled into writing on death certificates.

Which takes us back to the study of the Finnish lifters. Commenting on it in his newsletter *Figure Four*, Bryan Alvarez wrote that the range of their cases was "strikingly similar" to that of wrestlers: three suicides ... three heart attacks ... one likely drug-related coma ... one case of non-Hodgkin's lymphoma. Indeed, in the list below you will find brain aneurysms, suspicious cases of cancers of organs like the liver and the kidneys, and coronaries galore.

By way of perspective, wrestling historian J Michael Kenyon points out that the pro wrestler's "waltz with the nastier fates has been conducted at an accelerated rate from the get-go." What sent the numbers through the roof in our era has two clear proximate causes. The first is high-impact in-ring stunts; the end of "kayfabe," a coy suspension of disbelief in the bygone era, gave way to a can-you-top-this? mentality in the staging of matches. Contemporary daredevils either forgot, or blew right past, the caution that wrestling's head game was, in addition to being a tool to manipulate the masses, a form of self-preservation. Reaching back into carny dialect provides an apt description: many wrestlers today are "marks for themselves."

The second reason for of the high death rate, of course, is drugs. These in turn can be broken down, roughly, into the purely recreational variety (topped by cocaine – once defined by comic Robin Williams as "God's way of telling you that you're making too much money"); those designed to kill pain and/or induce sleep on the road; and physique- and performance-enhancers.

Some wrestling fatalities defy category. Here we highlight four of them.

• On July 17, 1988, Bruiser Brody (Frank Goodish), 42, was fatally stabbed in the stomach by another wrestler, The Invader (Jose Gonzales), in a dressing room in Bayamon, Puerto Rico. Gonzales, also the booker for the Puerto Rican promotion, was the last of a long list of wrestling authorities with whom "outlaw" Brody clashed, but the only one who chose to resolve their differences with a concealed hunting knife. Gonzales' claim of self-defense was refuted by at least one other mainland American wrestler who witnessed the attack, but potential witnesses were either intimidated from testifying or not adequately informed of the time and place of the trial. Gonzales thus was acquitted without taking the witness stand.

• On January 27, 1993, the heart of Andre the Giant (Andre Roussimoff), 46, gave out in a Paris hotel room. Andre's lifelong medical condition – acromegaly or "giantism," an overabundance of growth hormone – had both provided the source of his appeal to fans and fated him for early death. The analogy is crude, but some tall basketball players have been known to die from a medical condition called Marfan Syndrome.

• On May 23, 1999, Owen Hart, 33, whose wrestling character at that point was being called The Blue Blazer, was killed in Kansas City in an errant stunt fall – which was not part of an actual match and was caused by equipment failure – just before the start of a pay-per-view show. Hart's widow, Martha, subsequently settled a lawsuit against the then-World Wrestling Federation for $18 million.

• On May 1, 2003, Elizabeth Huelette, 42, a wrestling personality once known as The Lovely Elizabeth, choked to death while drinking alcohol and overdosing on pills in a suburban Atlanta home she shared with wrestler Lex Luger (Larry Pfohl). During her real-life marriage to Randy "Macho Man" Savage (Randy Poffo), which ended in divorce, Elizabeth had been Savage's storyline "valet" or "manager." Weeks prior to her death, Luger had been arrested on a report of a domestic disturbance; after her death he was arrested again on unrelated substance-abuse charges.

On to the list. Ideally, the format is WRESTLING NAME (REAL NAME), AGE, DATE OF DEATH, PLACE OF DEATH, CAUSE OF DEATH. In some entries, one or more elements are missing or unspecific. The rule of thumb was to include incomplete entries as long as the stated cause of death seemed well judged.

Jay Youngblood (real name Steve Romero), **30**. September 1, 1985. Australia. Pancreas failure following a match.

Rick McGraw, 30. November 1, 1985. New Haven, Connecticut. Heart attack.

Andrew "Bubba" Douglas, 42. February 13, 1986. Florida. Heart attack.

Gino Hernandez (real name Charles Wolfe), **29**. January 30, 1986. Texas. Cocaine overdose.

El Solitario (real name Roberto González Cruz), **39**. April 6, 1986. Heart attack.

Mike Von Erich (real name Michael Adkisson), **23**. April 12, 1987. Denton County, Texas. Suicide by overdosing on Placidyl (sleeping pills).

Scott "Hog" Irwin, 35. September 5, 1987. Minnesota. Brain aneurysm.

"Bad Bad" Leroy Brown (real name Leroy Rochester), **38**. September 6, 1988. Savannah, Georgia. Heart attack.

Ed "The Bull" Gantner, 31. December 31, 1990. Florida. Gun suicide. Both of his kidneys had failed due to steroid abuse.

Chief Thunder Mountain (real name David Mosier), **33**. August 1991. Heart attack.

Chris Von Erich (real name Chris Adkisson), **21**. September 12, 1991. Edom, Texas. Gun suicide.

Lance Idol (real name Steve Schuman), **32**. September 26, 1991. Heart disease.

"Mad Dog" Buzz Sawyer (real name Bruce Woyan), **32**. February 7, 1992. California. Cocaine overdose.

Kerry Von Erich (real name Kerry Adkisson), **33**. February 18, 1993. Shady Shores, Texas. Gun suicide.

Oro (real name Javier Hernandez), **21**. October 26, 1993. Mexico City. Brain aneurysm during a match.

Larry Cameron, 41. December 13, 1993. Germany. Heart attack during a match.

Ray Candy (real name Raymond Canty), **43**. May 23, 1994. Decatur, Georgia. Heart attack.

Tiny Anderson (real name Russell Knorr), **42**. 1994. Kidney failure.

Love Machine (previously billed as Beetlejuice; also wrestled under his real name, Art Barr), **28**. November 23, 1994. Springfield, Oregon. Heart failure perhaps brought on by alcohol and painkillers.

Tiny Anderson (real name Russell Knorr), **42**. January 1995. Kidney failure.

Jerry "Crusher" Blackwell, 45. January 22, 1995. Georgia. Pneumonia.

"Hot Stuff" Eddie Gilbert, 33. February 18, 1995. San Juan, Puerto Rico. Heart attack.

Big John Studd (real name John Minton), **47.** March 20, 1995. Liver cancer, Hodgkin's Disease.

"Mr. America" Don Ross (also billed as Ripper Savage), **48.** June 2, 1995. Heart attack.

Black Venus (real name Jean Kirkland), **47.** September 29, 1995. Heart attack.

Dick Murdoch, 49. June 15, 1996. Amarillo, Texas. Heart attack.

Neil Superior (real name Neil Caricofe), **33.** August 23, 1996. Ocean City, Maryland. Died in a long, wild altercation with police. The pathologist ruled the nature of the death as "undetermined" and the cause as "multiple drug use & arteriosclerotic cardiovascular disease."

Big City Mike (real name Rick Martello), **38.** January 3, 1997. Heart failure.

Plum Mariko (real name Mariko Umeda), **29,** August 16, 1997. Hiroshima, Japan. Brain aneurysm from a blow to the head during a match.

Jeep Swenson (real name Robert Swenson), **40.** August 19, 1997. Los Angeles. Heart attack.

Brian Pillman, 35. October 5, 1997. Bloomington, Minnesota. Heart attack, probably brought on by drug use.

Big E Sleaze (real name Jeremy Sumpter), **22**. October 26, 1997. Maryland. Gun suicide.

Louie Spiccoli (real name Louis Mucciolo), **27**. February 15, 1998. San Pedro, California. Asphyxiation. Found choked on his own vomit after ingesting large quantities of alcohol mixed with the painkiller Carisopradol (also known as soma).

Larry "Lucha" Doyal, 37, June 21, 1998. California. Complications from diabetes.

Shane Shamrock (real name Brian Hauser), **22**. August 18, 1998. Maryland. Shot by police during a domestic disturbance.

Dan Curtis, 37. December 29, 1998. Heart attack.

Emiko Kado, 23. April 9, 1999. Fukota, Japan. Brain injury from a bad bump during a match.

"Ravishing" Rick Rude (real name Richard Rood), **41**. April 20, 1999. Alpharetta, Georgia. Heart attack. A bottle of prescription pain pills was found by his side. The medical examiner said he overdosed on "mixed medications." Rude had testified to his abuse of steroids.

The Renegade (real name Richard Wilson), **33**. February 23, 1999. Marietta, Georgia. Gun suicide.

Yuel Lovett (real name Alex Lovett), **28**. July 31, 1999. Peru. Heart attack.

Brian Hildebrand, 37. September 8, 1999. Talbot, Tennessee. Stomach cancer.

Kronnus (real name Sergio Armando Villa), **27**, September 15, 1999. Mexico City. Stabbed near the arena.

Tony Rumble (real name Anthony Magliaro), **43**. November 13, 1999. Heart attack.

Mr. Ebony (real name Steven Caster), **46**. December 19, 1999. Heart attack.

Gary Albright, 36. January 7, 2000. Hazleton, Pennsylvania. Heart attack during a match.

Bobby Duncum Jr., 34. January 24, 2000. Austin, Texas. Overdose on painkillers mixed with alcohol.

Masakazu Fukuda, 27. April 19, 2000. Tokyo. Cerebral hemorrhage from a blow in the ring.

Jumbo Tsuruta (real name Tomomi Tsuruta), **49**. May 13, 2000. Manila, Philippines. Complications from liver surgery.

Harlem Warlord (Jaime Cardiche), **32**. July 28, 2000. In surgery.

Tony Nash, 30. August 5, 2000. Milwaukee. Ring injury.

Chris Duffy, 36. August 25, 2000. Seizure.

Canadian Destroyer (real name Douglas Chevalier), **41**. September 10, 2000. Ontario, Canada. Heart attack.

Yokozuna (real name Rodney Anoia), **34**. October 23, 2000. Liverpool, England. Heart attack.

Rick Bolton, 49. December 5, 2000. Chatham, Ontario, Canada. Heart attack.

Sombra Negra (Edward Ortiz Torres), **30**. June 1, 2001. Heart attack.

Terry "Bam Bam" Gordy, 40, July 16, 2001. Soddy Daisy, Tennessee. Heart attack.

Monster Ripper (real name Rhonda Sing), **40**. July 27, 2001. Calgary, Alberta, Canada. Suicide.

Russ Haas, 27. December 15, 2001. Cincinnati. Heart attack.

Mike Davis, 46. December 25, 2001. Dallas. Heart failure.

Jeff "Rattlesnake" Raitz, 38. February 9, 2002. Heart attack.

Big Dick Dudley (real name Alex Rizzo), **37**. May 16, 2002. Copiague, New York. Kidney failure brought on by painkillers.

The British Bulldog ("Davey Boy" Smith), **39**, May 18, 2002. Invermere, British Columbia, Canada. Heart attack.

Billy Joe Travis (Gary Mize), November 22, 2002. London, Kentucky. Heart attack.

Curt Hennig (also billed as "Mr. Perfect"), **44**. February 9, 2003. Brandon, Florida. Acute cocaine intoxication.

Kodo Fuyuki, 42. March 19, 2003. Japan. Cancer.

"Bullwhip" Danny Johnson, 49. July 20, 2003. Hamilton, Ontario, Canada. Kidney and liver failure.

Joe Powers (real name Roy Bradbury), **41**. September 3, 2003. Roanoke, Virginia. Liver disease.

Anthony "Pitbull II" Durante, 36. September 24, 2003. Overdose of the pain drug Oxycontin.

Road Warrior Hawk (real name Michael Hegstrand), **45**. October 19, 2003. Indian Rocks Beach, Florida. Heart attack.

Floyd Creatchman, 46. October 25, 2003. Montreal. Crohn's Disease (inflammation of the digestive tract).

Crash Holly (real name Michael Lockwood), **34**. November 6, 2003. Navarre, Florida. Choked on a pool of his own vomit and blood; believed to have overdosed on more than 90 Carisopradol (soma) pills.

Jerry Tuite (variously billed as The Wall, Malice, and Gigantes), **36**. December 5, 2003. Tokyo, Japan. Heart attack.

Mike Lozanski, 35. December 18, 2003. Calgary, Canada. Believed to be from a heart condition or fluid in the lungs.

Danny Fargo (real name Audie Hager), **44**. December 26, 2003. Nicholasville, Kentucky. Heart attack.

Hercules (real name Ray Fernandez), **47**. March 6, 2004. Tampa, Florida. Heart attack.

Victor The Bodyguard (real name Victor M. Rodriguez Garcia), **38**. June 20, 2004. Yauco, Puerto Rico. Heart attack.

Big Bossman (real name Ray Traylor), **42**. September 23, 2004. Dallas, Georgia. Heart attack.

Marianna Komlos, **35**. September 26, 2004. Prince George, British Columbia, Canada. Breast Cancer.

El Texano (real name Juan Jauregui), **47**. January 15, 2005. Guadalajara, Mexico. Lung and respiratory failure.

Chris Candido (real name Christopher Candito), **33**. April 28, 2005. Matawan, New Jersey. Blood clot caused by complications from leg surgery. Blood clots are a common side effect of steroids.

The Spider (real name Dan Quirk), **22**. May 28, 2005. Taunton, Massachusetts. Head trauma after a missed move during a match.

Shinja Hashimoto, 40. July 11, 2005. Yokohama, Japan. Brain aneurysm.

Eddie Guerrero, 38. November 13, 2005. Minneapolis. Heart failure, brought on by high levels of steroids and narcotics.

Lord Humongous (real name Emory Hail), **36**. January 29, 2006. St. Petersburg, Florida. Kidney failure.

Johnny Grunge (real name Michael Durham), **39**. February 26, 2006. Peachtree City, Georgia. Complications from sleep apnea.

Earthquake (real name John Tenta), **42**, June 7, 2006. Friendswood, Texas. Bladder cancer.

Tiger Khan (real name Marlon Kalkai), **33**, June 26, 2006. Los Angeles. Heart attack.

Billy Firehawk (real name William J. Hawkins III), **40**, July 17, 2006. Quebec, Canada. Complications from diabetes.

Jimmy "Hustler" Alicea, 33, November 21, 2006. Brooklyn, New York. Heart attack.

ACKNOWLEDGMENTS

In publishing terms, I was working the equivalent of indie shows in high school gyms when Michael Holmes of ECW PRESS took an interest in my writing. I'm grateful to Michael both for that and for his wise judgment on the photos and production elements that make the book you are holding an attractive package. Michael happens to be an accomplished poet as well as an able editor of "misFit" books — which means that he basically has all the brows of North American culture surrounded. I suggest that the editors of the so-called major publishing houses "tap out" to him without delay.

I was introduced to Michael by Larry Matysik, whom wrestling fans will remember as the program editor, booker, television and house show ring announcer, and all-purpose executive associate for my late uncle, Sam Muchnick, the St. Louis promoter and National Wrestling Alliance president. (Larry had just written a terrific book of his own for ECW PRESS about these experiences, *Wrestling at the Chase: The Inside Story of Sam Muchnick and the Legends of Professional Wrestling*. Simultaneously with my book, Larry is coming out with his second, a biography of Bruiser Brody in collaboration with Brody's widow Barbara.) After my uncle retired in 1982 and the business took its historic turns, Larry became my No. 1 pipeline for information about it. Much more important is that Larry is my very good friend.

Dave Meltzer, publisher of the *Wrestling Observer Newsletter*, has forgotten more about wrestling than I'll ever know. There, I just said it again . . . now, where are my royalties? Since 1984 Dave also has been generous with his expertise, often taking time from his own killer production schedule to read and comment on my pre-publication drafts. I thank him for that — and for not cutting me off after I publicly ribbed him about his propensity for comma splices and run-on sentences. Seriously, Meltzer's output of reporting and analysis, week upon year upon decade, has been amazing.

Other "kayfabe sheet" journalists have been helpful, too, from time to time. Wade Keller, of *Pro Wrestling Torch*, merits singling out. Dave Scherer, of 1wrestling.com and more recently prowrestlinginsider.com, also has pointed me in helpful directions more than once. While I claim complete personal credit for all the brilliant and original interpretations and insights herein, it goes without saying that any possible errors of fact are the exclusive responsibility of people like Meltzer, Keller, and Scherer.

In alphabetical order, here are some of the other folks who provided critical support of various kinds over the years: Dan Bischoff, Dave Brooks, Jack Heidenry, Pat Heidenry, Mark Lasswell, Jim Leeson, Barbara Moulton, Phil Mushnick, Andrew O'Hehir, Howard Orenstein, Randy Shaw, Joel Simon, Andrew Stuart, Alice Sunshine, Kim Wood.

I apologize to anyone I omitted. And I especially apologize to those on the list who wish they had been omitted.

Irvin Muchnick
Berkeley, California
November 2006

ABOUT THE AUTHOR

Irvin Muchnick has written about media, business, higher education, and nice clean sports — as well as pro wrestling — for many major magazines and newspapers. A native of St. Louis, he lives in California with his wife and four children. In his last wrestling match, in junior high school, he broke his right collarbone.

Photo Credits

Corbis: page 46.
The Mike Lano Collection: page 18, 58, 62, 70, 76, 86, and 138.
The Bob Leonard Collection: page 121.
The Larry Matysik Collection: page 2, 6, 9, 14, and 22.
The Dewey Robertson Collection: page 20.

All other photographs are from the ECW Press wrestling photo archive.